The Power of Compassion

D1215772

Paulist Press † New York/Ramsey

The Power of Compassion

— by —

James McNamara

Library of Congress
Catalog Card Number:
83-62463

ISBN:
0-8091-2567-6

Published by Paulist Press
545 Island Road
Ramsey, N.J. 07446

Printed and bound in the
United States of America

Contents

To my parents
Joseph and May McNamara.
As they live now in the peace and
compassion of Christ
may the wisdom
of God be theirs
in the abundance
they richly deserve.

Introduction

The experience of being powerless, of not making a difference, the feeling of helplessness, of being overwhelmed and overwrought, is an all too frequent and very tragic description of the lives of many people in this age of nuclear madness. The experience of powerlessness frustrates men and women at every turn. The economy with its double-digit inflation outdistances even the power brokers, burdens the middle class, and crushes the poor. The rise in unemployment leaves no one immune from its web of helplessness and despair. The increase of crime and violence in our society (itself an indication of the explosiveness of powerlessness) paralyzes people in fear and retribution. And then there is the awareness that even as we live and breathe weapons are pointed at our destruction, nuclear weapons that could annihilate us and our entire civilization in a matter of minutes. While we focus our fears on enemies without, we fail to appreciate the destructive influence of the mere presence of these weapons upon a generation of young people who feel powerless to even entertain a future and who all too quickly and pervasively abandon themselves to the meaninglessness of the moment.

Innocence is related to this experience of powerlessness and also characterizes the times in which we live. This innocence does not take account of evil and fails to name evil for what it truly is. This is the innocence that sees evil outside but

1

never within, that sees evil in others but doesn't recognize the evil in oneself. Such innocence leads to self-righteousness when one expects everyone and everything to be perfect and then fails to deal with the complexities of very real situations whether they be personal or international. It is the innocence that justifies evil in the name of something good. I will attempt to be more specific and concrete in later sections of this book. For now I invite you to investigate with me the notion that forms the basis of these reflections: Powerlessness and innocence are adversaries of spirituality. I invite you to search out its truthfulness and its limitations.

I begin with the conviction that the human drama is lived out in the context of mystery, something that defies explanation, that is beyond human comprehension. St. Augustine once defined preaching as mystery speaking to mystery about Mystery. Each person is a mystery—you to me, me to you, and each of us to ourselves. The source of our identity, our origin, is grounded in mystery. These convictions do not dampen my spirits by obfuscating matters or lead me to believe that this investigation is fruitless. Rather, the presence of mystery immerses me in an exciting and challenging search within myself and in my experience to discern the reality of truth and the presence of meaning in the human adventure. I invite you to allow your own experience to shed light upon the reflections that form this investigation.

Finally, I invite you to enter into these reflections within the perspective of the centrality of compassion. I will begin with some reflections on my personal journey in the direction of compassion. These moments for compassion are an essential background to everything I wish to say in the subsequent pages. It is compassion that leads me beyond powerlessness and innocence as adversaries of spirituality and into the experience of the cross of Christ where both powerlessness and innocence become virtues through personal surrender to the call of the Father.

I. Moments for Compassion

Three years ago my spiritual director of many years died suddenly. He was a very gifted priest, a real man of the Lord. Throughout his life, but especially in retirement, he had developed an effective ministry in letter writing. When he died I felt the urge to follow his example in reaching out to people through correspondence. Some friends suggested I pray about an appropriate Scripture that could form a letterhead. I chose a brief line from the Epistle of James: "The wisdom of God is full of compassion" (Jas 3:17). I regard compassion as perhaps the most important conversion of my life. This conversion is not a one-time event or a static reality. It is, rather, a whole process, a direction in which I find myself still immersed. It began sometime in the seminary but did not really bear fruit until the early days of parish life. It moved me from the distance of judgment to the oneness of understanding. I still have far to go, and I do not move in just a positive direction but vacillate back and forth, especially vulnerable to judgment when I am angry. I would like to offer some personal reflections on that journey and point to experiences that had a deep impact upon me, moving me in the direction of compassion.

I had the fortune of growing up in a family that provided a lot of joy and security. I am the youngest of three children. My German-American mother instilled in us a deep sense of honesty and perseverance. My Irish-American father gave us a cheerful spirit and a positive feeling for people. I presumed that everyone grew up the way I did, had the same opportunities, and was given the same values. When I became a priest and became involved in the lives of the people in the parish, I was overwhelmed by the brokenness and the pain that I encountered. From 1971 to 1978 I was very privileged to live in a parish that was filled with many generous Christian people, people who in both their joys and their sorrows had a profound effect upon me and taught me volumes about being a man and a Christian. Many of those people are still my friends today; many hold a special place in my heart and my memory because of the moments we shared together.

What follows are some key events in the course of my first year there. These events are each rather extraordinary in their own right and may seem overwhelming when put together. They are important not only because they happened to me in that brief period of time. They are also important because they had a profound effect upon me. In between these events were very ordinary day to day experiences that were valuable and influential in their own subtle way, experiences that in themselves called for compassion and would lead to compassion. But, because of the secure and somewhat sheltered nature of my own upbringing, these dramatic events were able to affect me in ways that ordinary experiences were not able to do. These dramatic moments were able to open me to a world of pain and fear, to a world of feeling and emotion that drew me into the drama of life as a participant instead of an observer, as a fellow traveler instead of a judge. A dialectic was to develop between these tragic events and the everyday call to compassion and love. Let us first look at these events and then at their daily implications.

From the very beginning I found myself confronted with the anguish of people's lives. The very first day I was on duty I was called to the hosptial to anoint a man who was badly burned in a gas explosion. The scene in the emergency room is indelibly etched in my mind. The older curate, sensitive to my newness and inexperience, was very kind in going with me to the hospital. That was in June 1971. In August of that year a policeman was killed when he interrupted a holdup in Queens while on his way to work. He left his wife and seven children ranging in age from fifteen months to seventeen years. I did not know them well at the time, but when I saw them at the early morning Mass the next day, I went and sat in the pew. It was awful to sit there and feel so helpless, so powerless. They were all crying and there wasn't anything to be said that could take away their pain. But something was beginning to happen to me that was important. I was beginning to feel some of their pain. I who had experienced so much security and joy growing up, I who thought that everyone's life was like mine, found myself devastated by this tragic in-breaking of their lives.

I concelebrated at the funeral Mass which was said by a priest friend of the family, a very compassionate and kind Irishman whom I truly respected for his presence to and care for these people. The funeral was attended by several thousand policemen and dignitaries from city and state. After going to the cemetery, I returned to the rectory where some of the policemen were being served lunch provided by the Police Department. I was about to join them when the phone rang and the family asked me to come and have lunch at their home. I was very struck by the contrast in the two scenes. At the house there were a few relatives and friends as compared to the hundreds who were crowded into the field behind the rectory. And I realized ever so poignantly that much as we all felt deeply saddened by the death of this good man, his children and his wife were the ones who really had to bear the loss and live with the implications of his death.

That evening, as chance would have it, I was the only one home for dinner in the rectory. There's always something lonely about eating alone, and on this particular day I found it painful. As I sat there nibbling at my food, tears were streaming down my face. I thought to myself, "My God, you're losing your mind. You're letting this get to you too much. You can't take on so much pain." Yet I couldn't help but feel the devastation this family was experiencing. And I thought it was so unfair that their lives should be so shattered. Indeed I had been very fortunate in my life. I thought of the statement in Luke's Gospel (something I have thought of many times since): "To him to whom much is given much will be required" (Lk 12:48).

This pain I was experiencing was not a bad thing. It led me to compassion; it motivated me to care about these beautiful people. A few days later I stopped to say hello but no one was home. As I started to leave, I heard some young voices calling my name. The family lived on a canal; eleven year old Brian and nine year old Glenn were just going out in their small boat. They invited me to come along. I grew up in a land-locked Hicksville, and not only had I rarely been in a boat but I couldn't swim, so the thought of getting into this little dinghy with these two little guys caused me great anxiety. However, pride and their appealing request led me to abandon the afternoon to this venture. It was the beginning of many such moments with these very special and courageous people who were so important to the early years of my priesthood.

There was the time that Glenn told me he was going to capsize the boat and hurl me into the water. And despite my best threats, he did it. And there was the time when Kevin was a senior at La Salle Military Academy and needed someone to give him his senior officer's pin at the Father's Day Parade. I can still remember the tremendous feeling of meaning and joy inside of me when he asked me to come to the school and take part in the ceremony. What a great privilege to stand in another man's shoes and do something symbolically important for his son. I don't think I have ever felt more deeply the privilege of being a Christian and of being a priest. They are all grown up now and don't need me to do these things for them anymore. But I still enjoy seeing them and I will always be grateful to them for what they taught me in so many simple human ways about the power of compassion.

Another very tragic incident forms another dimension to my journey with compassion. It has more to do with my own failing and inadequacy than the previous story. In November 1971 there was a serious auto accident in our village. Four teenagers in one car crashed head-on with a car containing three adults. Three of the teenagers were killed. It was 11:00 P.M. on a Friday night when I was called to the hospital. A nurse brought me into a darkened room that contained the bodies of the three teenagers. As we came out of the room three adults were walking hurriedly toward us down the hall: a man and two women. A policeman began whispering in my ear: "Tell the woman on the right that her daughter is in the X-ray room. And the couple, that's their son and daughter who were killed." Somehow I was to transmit this information to those people who were obviously upset.

The doctor present looked for a room where this couple could sit down and be told this awful news. It took several minutes to unlock a conference room during which time the parents became more agitated. Finally, they were seated and the nurse, the doctor, and the policeman looked at me. I was frozen, almost paralyzed, as I looked at them. I couldn't speak. I began to stutter. The father asked in anguish, "Why can't I see my kids?" And I blurted out, "Because they're dead." The couple were understandably upset. We stayed with them for over an hour. Then I was called to see some of the other people who were injured in the crash. After some time I discovered that the couple were leaving, planning to drive home alone. They lived several towns away, so I ran out to the parking lot and offered to drive them home. I couldn't see how they could drive home alone but they insisted and went home to tell their daughter what had happened. I stayed at the hospital until 3:00 A.M. waiting for the parents of the third teenager, but they were out of town.

From the time I had arrived at the hospital I discovered that I was expected to bear the responsibility of communicating the tragic news of this event. Doctors and nurses went about their work of binding wounds, and they did so with competence. The police filled out reports and tried to sort out exactly what happened. But the communication of this news and its meaning, the burden of the question "Why?", was left totally in my hands. At twenty-six I felt quite inadequate and powerless. I went home but didn't sleep the rest of the night nor the next night. I felt like such a failure. I felt that I had let these people down. If there was a compassionate way to tell them such terrible news, I didn't find it. If there was a professional way, I didn't succeed.

To my surprise, the phone rang on Sunday afternoon and a relative of the parents said that the couple would like me to come to the funeral parlor. When I arrived that evening the place was filled with people. The parents met me at the door and walked with me down a long hall to the room where the wake was being held. As we moved along I could hear people saying, "Oh, that must be him." "Yes, that's probably the priest". I had a feeling of dread inside of me. What are they saying? What do they mean? "That's that incompetent who bungled it the other night?" Well, I soon began to realize what they meant, and it was a lesson in priesthood I will never forget. In their eyes, which were eyes of faith, I was the one who brought the compassion of God, his blessing, his peace, to their children. This meant a great deal to them. And the fact that I couldn't speak, that I stuttered, was understandable to them because I was human and I cared enough to feel deeply the tragedy that I was called upon to reveal to them.

I learned something about St. Paul's conviction that in weakness power reaches perfection, that when I am weak it is then that I am strong. I ended up saying the funeral Mass and saw the parents for several years after this. Even now, over a decade later, I hear from them occasionally. We are good for each other because we help to heal each other's wounds. They taught me a lot about the power of compassion.

That first year of priesthood I felt bombarded with the pain and brokenness of others. In addition to these tragic events I was listening to teenagers being torn apart by the alcoholism in their home or the disintegration of their parents' relationship. I was listening to parents struggling to be faithful or to find meaning in their lives of emptiness and routine. What I had thought was a big argument when growing up at home was nothing compared to the tensions and divisions I was discovering. What I thought was a major problem was minor in comparison to the burdens some of these people were carrying.

In June as that year came to a close, we had a party for the teachers in religious education on a Friday night and I got to bed very late. The next day I had to preach at a Mass for Dominican sisters, and so in the afternoon I hid in my room to rest awhile and prepare my talk. I was not on duty and I asked the secretary to take messages. About a half hour later she buzzed me and said that there was a man to see a priest and the priest on duty was busy. The worst message you can get over the intercom is that message. If they are there to see a priest, they don't particularly want to see you, and if they are there unannounced they could want anything from having a medal blessed to presenting a big problem.

In the office I met a young black man named Charlie. I sat down filled with prejudice: he probably wants money. I'm not on duty, I'm tired and deserve some rest. Charlie started to tell a tale of woe, of being unemployed, rejected. I quickly suggested that he needed professional help and that I would be happy to refer him to a counselor. If he would just sit there a minute I would look up some names and phone numbers. When I came back he was gone. I went out the front door and saw him heading down to the village. I went back to my room but I couldn't relax. I began to realize how cold and abrupt I had been with him. I didn't listen. I didn't care about him. I only cared about myself and my desire to be in control of my day. I wasn't in touch with the very real evil inside of me that led me to be so selfish and blind. I got in the car and went to look for Charlie. I drove all over town for an hour but couldn't find him. I returned to the rectory only to become more restless remembering how he talked about suicide because nobody cared.

I prayed and asked the Lord to help me find Charlie not for his sake but for mine because I had failed and wanted a second chance. I went out again and found Charlie walking along a side street. He wouldn't acknowledge me. I was driving along on the wrong side of the street. Finally I pulled into a driveway into his path and asked him to forgive me. I tried to explain why I was wrong and asked him to give me a second chance. He told me that I was just like everyone else, that nobody cared and nobody wanted to listen. He turned and walked away and I never saw him again. By now, I was due to say Mass for the sisters, but now I had a homily—all about Charlie and myself.

At the end of that year I wrote a letter to my spiritual director—that elderly man filled with wisdom and grace. He wrote back a brief note that contained a rather striking statement: "If I were asked to form a young priest, I would break his heart." That's not what I wanted to hear at the time but it has come to mean a great deal to me. It is, for me, the way to conversion and it occurs through compassion.

The years ahead were to bring many other dramatic moments—moments for compassion. I would be called upon to bless six family victims of a mass murder and celebrate their funeral Mass. In one week of September 1976, I would be called to minister to four victims burned to death in a plane crash, anoint a man who drowned at the beach, and sit in vigil for a teenage girl who slowly died of a gunshot wound. When the teenager who worked in the rectory was diagnosed with Hodgkin's disease I went over to church and sat there for quite a while before going to the house to see my young friend. One of his friends came into church and said, "What are you doing here? I've been trying to track you down." I told him that I had to deal with some of my own feelings before I could deal with everyone else. I was hurt and angry and I had to talk to the Lord about that.

These events had important influences upon my daily experience of routine and mundane activities. The problem with compassion is not whether we are compassionate or not compassionate. The problem with compassion is that we are selective. We are compassionate with some people but not with others. We are filled with sympathy and feeling in some situations but not in others. We have compassion for the oppressed but not the oppressor—or the other way around. Our compassion can be selective in a temporal sense—when we are in the right mood or at the right time of the day for us.

Dramatic as these preceding stories are, their importance does not lie in the opportunity to be compassionate. Who would not be compassionate in such unusual circumstances? What is important about these events is their effect upon me, upon me as a young priest with a certain history, a particular way of looking at the world, and an accustomed emotional response to life. These happenings stopped the flow of life; they caused me to reflect, to look at myself and the world around me in a new way. Suddenly, time stopped and all else seemed trivial and unimportant in the light of this particular tragedy. I had to face the challenge of integrating these powerful events into my life and the everyday experiences of ministry. It is easy to say that, in the light of such tragedies, this particular person's problem is not very serious. There is a place for inviting people to put things in perspective, but that is usually the result of helping those persons to move ahead in their own life. It is rarely helpful when it is done out of my own impatience and intolerance.

Often, when people came to talk, they would begin with an apology: "I know you are very busy so I won't take much of your time." Or, even more directly: "I know there are people with worse problems and I shouldn't bother you, but there is something that has been troubling me." The point became clear to me that if it was important for them it was important, and that this was as much an opportunity for compassion and conversion for me as any other moment that made time stand still. The young mother who felt lonely and isolated at home raising small children wanted to find something meaningful to do to make her feel worthwhile as an adult. The middle-aged adult caught between two generations felt the pressure of coping with the unpredictability of teenagers and the dependency of an elderly parent. The teenagers and young adults were often confused about who they were and were struggling with the tangles of relationships in their lives. The elderly were often lonely and afraid. Some were peaceful and had a deep sense of God's presence in their lives. Some were still bearing the burdens of love in caring for younger generations. The single adults were asking questions about the meaning of their lives and the weight of their responsibilities in their profession and in their personal lives.

In the ordinary events of daily life people came to tell their story and wanted someone to listen. Compassion in these moments often meant the generosity and the courage to simply be there and listen. It required generosity because I usually had to let go of some project I was planning or moment of relaxation I was reserving for myself. This involved a conviction that these persons were important here and now, that their story, their problem or concern, was important to them and not to be judged or dismissed in comparison to the plight of others. And it required courage because there were often no solutions or answers. Despite these convictions, these encounters still came as interruptions and I usually went out to the office grumbling to myself about this intrusion into my day. Once again conversion became important to me. I had discovered the Jesus Prayer and had been using it in a mantra-like way in the more idle moments of my day. Now I began to use it before I went out to see someone in order to get in touch with something deeper inside me than my initial annoyance. "Lord Jesus Christ, have mercy on me a sinner." This simple prayer helps me to be a little more generous and courageous in listening to the people I meet.

The healing was often in the very act of being there and listening. That, in itself, became for me a conversion to compassion. "Can I speak with you a moment?" "Would you mind if . . . ?" "Can you give me a ride to the doctor?" "I have no one to go to the store for me." "I have no money to pay for the medicine I need." The examples are infinite. You may wish to fill in the picture from your own life. Perhaps for you it has been some tragic or dramatic event that has made time stand still and caused you to face some deep pain inside yourself or absorb the pain of another person. Or perhaps it has been the routine of life and your own fidelity to it that has formed you into Christ, into a compassionate, loving person. However that may be, all of us have before us many opportunities for compassion, provided that we are willing to look beyond ourselves and be open to what we see.

Parents are bombarded with moments of compassion every day. The litany of needs and requests that young children bring to each day is a continual challenge to parents to go beyond their own exhaustion or particular mood to be present to their children. Children are disarming in their transparency. They can see through us very easily. They are sensitive to the slightest change in our tone of voice or our bearing. I have discovered that it is easier to be an uncle than a parent. After a few hours of fun and games I can return to the safe refuge of my own home. A couple of years ago I took my three nephews away for a week. The youngest was four at the time. It was a great experience and I treasure the memories. But it was also an exhausting experience and an insight into the challenges parents face every day. The moments that called for compassion were often intricately tied to moments of exhaustion or exasperation.

Working people, in an office or a factory, married or single, are also bombarded with moments for compassion. Day after day they are rubbing elbows (and sometimes personalities) with the same people. Typical problems seem to pervade most places: who is not speaking to this or that person this week; what the latest gossip is; who works and who doesn't work; who gets stepped on and who does the stepping in order to get a promotion. Very often there is a great deal of talking about one another and little honest talking to one another. Such an atmosphere is a very difficult one in which to exercise compassion.

"If today you hear his voice harden not your hearts" (Ps 95). I can't be compassionate if I don't allow myself to be hurt. And I can't be compassionately present to others if I don't face that hurt prayerfully and in solitude. This involves the beautiful quality of compassion without which a Christian is not a Christian, and, perhaps most challenging of all, it involves the risk of being hurt not just once but over and over again.

Being hurt is not, in itself, the criterion of compassion. A willingness to be hurt is important to a willingness to be compassionate. Being hurt (the "broken heart" spoken of above) can lead to the opposite of compassion; it can create hardness of heart. This is particularly true when people have not been loved and cared for by others.

My own formative years provided me with much security and peace because of the experience of love and the opportunities to grow. One implication of this was that I lacked an appreciation of the plight of others and was prone to be judgmental. This is where the tragic moments recounted here became so important in my life. At the same time, the experience of being hurt could lead to compassion because I had experienced the love and support of family and friends. In this sense, the caring environment of my upbringing was to be the background that set the stage for growth in compassion.

II. Powerlessness and Innocence

I have come to articulate this notion that powerlessness and innocence are adversaries of spirituality from reading *Power and Innocence* by the psychotherapist and writer Dr. Rollo May. His book is subtitled, "A Search for the Sources of Violence." I find that what he has to say has many implications for spirituality as well as healthy human living. His book, which I read several times a few years ago, helped me to begin to name some of my own experience and my insight into the experience of other people trying to live an authentic and healthy spiritual life in our society today.

In the transition that has taken place in Catholicism since the Second Vatican Council one of the major shifts has been in the relationship between the Church and the world, between the believer and the surrounding world. This has been a shift from a faith that must be carefully guarded and kept safe from the contaminations of the world to a faith that is lived out in the world, challenged and hopefully strengthened through interaction with contemporary life. This has caused much pain and confusion on the part of people who grew up in one world and are now faced with another. Many grew up in a world that was intact, where everything was clear-cut, especially the lines between good and evil. We now live in a world where there is less certainty, where the gray area abounds, and where people are challenged to make decisions for themselves and think through their moral choices and commitments.

A second major shift has to do with how we experience the world. We live in a world that has become more interdependent economically and politically. Many of us grew up in a Church that emphasized personal responsibility in one's own interpersonal world. This is a necessary and important perspective, and one that is deeply ingrained in us. It is the perspective out of which this book is written. However, it can keep us from appreciating our corporate responsibility, our responsibility to examine our way of life and how it affects others, whether they be the poor who surround us or the oppressed who live far away. The area of social sin and the responsibility of the Christian to speak out against abuses by corporations and nations is an arena where many Christians prefer to remain pseudo-innocent partly because they feel powerless and partly because they are ingrained with a morality of personal responsibility that blinds them to these larger realities. Too often Catholics regard these critical issues (nuclear war, world hunger, corporation practices, etc.) as purely political and then object when the Church or Church leaders get involved. It is the responsibility of the Christian to be faithful to the Gospel of Jesus Christ and to apply that Gospel message to every area of life. Differences of opinion will exist as well as a plurality of approaches to these complex problems. It would be a step forward if Christians first recognize the moral and religious import of these important questions.

In the course of moving from a morality based on rules and regulations with an authority structure intact to a morality of conscience and personal responsibility Catholics have lost a sense of sin and of evil. Sin has been relegated to the forum of psychology where valid psychological insights have been abused to the point of negating evil and sin. Rationalization, intellectualization, blaming others, and finding excuses have provided people with opportunities to avoid a responsibility that is properly theirs. These psychological insights have shown us that people are not totally free, that they are influenced by their upbringing and history, that the human person is a complex of dynamic forces. In themselves these insights have been most valuable in helping us to understand the human person and the forces at work on him. They help us to appreciate the lack of freedom involved in human behavior. But they do not explain away evil or make sin an impossibility. Our sophistication has also led us naively to believe that evil does not exist because the explanation of a devil sitting on your shoulder and whispering alluring nothings in your ear is rather lacking.

All of this leads to an innocence that is false because it fails to take account of evil. Approaching the world with a naiveté that everything is good is an innocence that is an adversary of spirituality because it fails to deal with the reality of evil in our society today. The lack of a sense of one's own sinfulness and one's own capacity for evil is also a false innocence because it fails to appreciate the real human struggle between good and evil that is the stuff of a spiritual life.

The powerlessness that people feel today is connected to this pseudo-innocence. People do not think they make a difference—they feel unrecognized and unappreciated. This experience of powerlessness is very real for many people in our technological and impersonal society, and it is carried over into their personal lives. In my experience as a spiritual director I have discovered that the sense of powerlessness is a paralyzing experience for many people. The basic loss of a sense of one's own worth and value is at the heart of much of the blandness in the spirituality of people today. Because they don't think they have much to give, because they don't think they have power, they don't think they make much of a difference—for good or for evil. And so their lives are lived on a rather superficial, meaningless level that fails to come to grips with the drama of salvation, of the struggle between good and evil both within us and around us.

The popular notion "I'm O.K., you're O.K." has provided a healthy balance to the negativism of the past. But it has also been used to support an innocence and a powerlessness that is harmful to spiritual growth. In this age of positive thinking it is important to remember that it is O.K. not to be O.K. That's why Jesus Christ came as Savior and that's why we need him. There is a real crisis of faith today precisely because people fail to recognize their need for Jesus Christ, and they fail to recognize this need because they fail to recognize their own capacity for evil. If you don't think you are a sinner, you don't need Jesus Christ except as some social amenity or as the source of some superficial ethic. One of the main premises of this book comes from my experience: In the spiritual life it is as important to be in touch with your capacity for evil as it is to be in touch with your capacity for good.

Henry was a married man with several children, who had been coming to me for spiritual direction after having made a retreat. He was a good and sincere man who experienced an awakening, a beginning step to a spiritual life as a result of his retreat weekend. After the initial enthusiasm of such an experience, he settled into the routine of life with deeper convictions about prayer and the presence of the Lord. Then he went away for a week on a business trip and his life fell apart. He had an affair with a woman he met at this conference and came home desolate and confused. His wife noticed a change in him, a distancing and depression, but didn't know what was bothering him. He came to talk and told me he was thinking of leaving his wife and children and moving to another part of the country where his new friend lived. He was obviously in great pain and filled with great conflict. As I reflected upon him in later years, I realized he was typical of many men for whom this particular temptation is a likely trap. I have discovered over the years that a married man who is a very private person, who has intense feelings and emotions, and who has no friends with whom he can vent his problems is an easy prey to infidelity especially as the years pass and his relationship with his wife undergoes strain or adjustment.

Henry and I talked several times. He was not free and therefore not thinking very clearly or soundly. It was hard to make a breakthrough with him. Finally, one day he announced: "I've decided that one thing is clear. No matter what I do I always want Jesus to be part of my life." I responded spontaneously and directly: "Well, big deal! Isn't that exactly what is at stake here? Perhaps you can't have Jesus as part of your life if you deny him." That proved to be too much for him and he did not come to talk again for several months. He continued to come to Mass on Sundays but alone, separate from his family. He would sit on the side near the door and often wore sunglasses. He certainly was offering symbols of his situation. He did not see that his actions made a difference for good or evil. He did not recognize his powerlessness as an opportunity for the triumph of evil. But at least he was still coming to Mass.

One Sunday I was preaching about prayer and how we sometimes do not wish to pray because we may hear something we may not wish to hear. Catching my friend out of the corner of my eye, I went on to say that there are people here who do not want to talk to me because they do not want to hear what I have to say. He visibly stirred in his seat, and I feared that his one foot out of the Church would be joined by the other. However, that week he came to see me and told me that he had made a decision to remain with his family. I asked him what had turned the tide for him and I was very impressed with his answer. He spent hours alone riding a bicycle or walking around the neighborhood, and, in the silence he experienced, he began to touch what was deepest and most true inside himself. That led to a harmony not only within himself but with the

Lord. That harmony is still bearing fruit in his love for his family.

Definition and Description of Terms

In order to talk about powerlessness we must first talk about its opposite, its positive referent, namely, power. Rollo May defines power simply as "the ability to cause or prevent change."[1] Power can be seen as a potentiality, a possibility for future change or as an actuality, a possibility within me now. It is in this latter sense that Rollo May is using the term. Power is basically connected with being. The mere fact of my existence is a statement about power. I may not make full use of power, I may deny I have power, I may misuse power, but in the very givenness of being power exists. This is an important starting point. I will be distinguishing types of power and potential levels of power. I think it is important to recognize the presence of power from the very fact of being because the judgment that powerlessness is an adversary of spirituality is largely built upon the fact that powerlessness at its root is a denial of one's self, an impotency that does not allow for a spiritual life.

Surely there are situations where I am powerless—in affecting human relationships, in controlling the events of my life, in changing the structures of society and corporations. Surely there is much evidence to show that the experience of powerlessness is real. But to conclude from this that human beings are devoid of power is to confuse fact with substance. The fact that human beings are powerless in given situations, or even in many situations, does not mean that human beings are powerless as such. Powerlessness, as a failure to recognize that one possesses power simply because one exists, is an adversary of spirituality because it fails to recognize both the potential for good and the effect of evil.

In this book I am using the term "power" as distinct though not divorced from the term "force." Force is the lowest common denominator of power and is usually identified with power. In the real world in which we live, force is a reality to be reckoned with as an element of power. But in talking here about power and powerlessness I am not primarily concerned about the use of force. I am primarily concerned about power in a more personal sense, what Rollo May calls a "sense of significance." This type of power refers "to a person's conviction that he counts for something, that he has an effect on others, and that he can get recognition from others."[2] May distinguishes five kinds of power, all of which are present in the same person at the same time and all of which are experienced in desire and in action. When people deny the use of these kinds of power in the name of powerlessness they leave themselves prey to the workings of evil—hence allowing powerlessness to become an adversary of spirituality.

The first is exploitative power. May describes this as the simplest and most destructive kind of power. It identifies power with force as in the example of slavery where one person holds power over the body and indeed the entire person of another. Manipulative power is similar to exploitative power in that it is power over another but involves in some way (through manipulation) the cooperation of the other. "Manipulative power may have originally been invited by the person's own destruction or anxiety."[3] Competitive power is power against another. Here one's rise depends upon another's fall. There are positive aspects to this type of power. "To have someone against you is not necessarily a bad thing: at least he is not over you or under you, and accepting his rivalry may bring out dormant capacities in you."[4]

The other two types of power are positive and constructive. Nutrient power is power for the other, as in parents' care for children. Integrative power is power with the other person.

This type of power sees the participants as equals who interact in such a way that growth takes place. Hegel's dialectical notion of thesis, antithesis, and synthesis expresses the process of integrative power that leads to growth. All these forms of power, both the destructive and the constructive, flow from the person's sense of his or her own significance or insignificance. How one experiences one's own power of being, how one appreciates or fails to appreciate who one is, and how one is able or unable to articulate oneself are all personal questions about power that determine one's use of any of these kinds of power. I will go into this in greater detail in a later section on the cry for significance.

Rollo May uses Martin Luther King's notion of non-violence as an example of integrative power. His example is useful not only in regard to the use of power but in understanding the difference between authentic innocence and pseudo-innocence. King states that his method "has a way of disarming the opponent. It exposes his moral defenses. It weakens his morale and at the same time it works on his conscience. He just doesn't know how to handle it."[5] That this is a use of power is most important to recognize. When non-violence is not seen as a use of power it is an example of pseudo-innocence. Whenever power is used and unrecognized, it runs the distinct danger of being destructive because it lacks the reflectiveness and awareness that should characterize human action. When recognized for what it is, the power of non-violence can be effective of its intention—"to work on the conscience." When it is not recognized for what it is, the power of non-violence can simply be the catalyst for violence. Its pseudo-innocence leads to surprise and self-righteousness for being the victim of violence instead of seeing itself as the cause. This pseudo-innocence refuses to own the effect it is having upon another person or group of persons. It refuses to own its shadow and the shadow that exists in the other. Rollo May sums this up well:

The authentic innocence of the non-violent person is the source of his power. The genuine rather than the pseudo-quality of the innocence is attested by the facts, first, that the non-violence does not involve any blocking off of awareness. Second, it does not involve the renouncing of responsibility. Third, its purpose is not to gain something for the individual himself but for his community, be it the nation of India or a community of blacks.[6]

The word "innocence" literally means not harmful, to be free from guilt or sin, guileless, pure. In actions it means without evil influence or effect, or not arising from evil intentions.[7] Rollo May distinguishes two kinds of innocence. The first is a quality of the imagination, the innocence of the artist or poet. It is the preservation of a childlike clarity in adulthood. "It is the preservation of childlike attitudes into maturity *without sacrificing* the realism of one's *perception of evil.*"[8] My italics underscore a key notion of an innocence that does lead to spirituality precisely because it does not ignore evil. The other kind of innocence does not lead to spirituality but consists of blinders. The pseudo-innocence is a childishness rather than a childlikeness. Instead of dealing with the complexity of a problem a person hides behind powerlessness and weakness, making them virtues. This type of innocence paints its own acceptable picture of reality (its own utopia) and misses (does not want to see) the real dangers.

A story may help clarify this point. Two men once worked together. One was naive while the other was of a suspicious nature. They had much to learn from each other. They worked for a man who was, on the one hand, cunning, manipulative and deceptive. On the other hand, this man in charge was also a nervous and fear-filled person. A victim of the "Peter Principle," he had long since risen to his level of incompetence. The subordinates experienced him as a good man who did bad things. They would meet together and decide upon a certain course of action. The next thing the subordinates knew, everything was changed and they were "had." Mr. Naiveté would say, "We'll have to go and talk with him again. I don't think he understood." Mr. Suspicion would reply, "He understood all right. He just chose to ignore us and do as he pleased." A few go-arounds on this and Mr. Naiveté began to see that his boss was indeed playing games with him. He would continually be shocked and disappointed because he refused to believe there was evil involved. Evil had to bite him before he would admit it existed. The evil, at least as it was perpetrated by the boss, was not a malicious evil. It was the result of the man's own limitations and fears, but it was still evil and needed to be dealt with as such. "It is this innocence that cannot come to terms with the destructiveness in oneself or others. . . . Innocence that cannot include the daimonic becomes evil."[9] Innocence that cannot include the daimonic is evil and thus an adversary of spirituality.

How then might we define spirituality? Spirituality is the struggle between good and evil. Spirituality begins with the recognition that man is spirit, embodied spirit, that man is a spirit in the world. Spirituality assents to the notion that there is a transcendent quality to a human person, a quality that enables a person to think, to reflect, to hope, to dream. Spirituality is not a life apart. It is my life being lived out in the world of space and time, in the midst of incompleteness, of evil, and of sin. The struggle between good and evil that characterizes the spiritual life includes the struggle between relative goods, between good and not so good. In this broken world of ours it is important to recognize that goodness is fragile and evil is all too real.

Present Day Society: America's View of Itself

I would like to show that one of the crises facing American society has to do with an image of itself that at base is caught up in pseudo-innocence. There are many reasons that one could point to (e.g., materialism and narcissism) that explain America's spiritual depravity, but I would like to focus on America's pseudo-innocence as one important contribution. The three symbols of the Garden of Eden, the Chosen People, and the Statue of Liberty may help explicitate America's view of itself.

The original founders of our country came to establish a land built on the high ideals of freedom, tolerance, and justice. Their search was also a turning away from a land that they had experienced as unjust, intolerant, and enslaved. There was a pseudo-innocence in their view of themselves that has haunted America ever since. If you are the Chosen People who set out to establish the perfect society you can see your cause as pure and good and see everything else as an obstacle and therefore as evil. And so it becomes justifiable to exterminate the "savages" in order to establish this democratic society. The Garden of Eden myth comes at a high price. In all war and violence, people, the enemy, are reduced to sub-human status in order to justify what in reality is evil. The Indians are seen as savages and thus lose the right of being treated as persons. Those who disagree are not tolerated. Evil unrecognized becomes evil unchecked.

The height of pseudo-innocence is to see one's self-interest as equal to the will of God. Whatever the Chosen People do in service of the perfect society, the Garden of Eden, is justified because it furthers what God wants. Here pseudo-innocence lacks the awareness and the responsibility that would bring itself to task. Innocence that sees evil only existing outside oneself (in the past one is running away from, as in the flight from the intolerance and the injustice of Europe, or in the obstacles one finds in one's path, as in the presence of the Indians in the new land) is an innocence that carries an evil even more potent than the evil it fled. This pseudo-innocence has blinders that are more selective than the pseudo-innocence spoken of above.

Unlike that innocence that failed to appreciate the presence of evil anywhere, this innocence refuses to appreciate the presence of evil within and projects it all outward. In one sense it comes down to power, the power of being, and how one sees oneself. An America that claims to leave power on its European shores ends up an America distrustful of power. Look at the attempts to balance power in our Constitution. An America that sees itself as the Chosen People come to establish the Garden of Eden ends up an America festering with violence. Look at the high rate of violent crime in our country compared to Europe.

The Statue of Liberty is also a symbol that allows America to see itself in an unhealthy innocent way.

> Give me your tired, your poor,
> your huddled masses, yearning
> to breathe free, the wretched
> refuse of your teeming shore,
> Send these, the homeless,
> tempest-tossed to me. I lift my
> lamp beside the golden door.

The ideals are noble and noteworthy. But the innocence is false because, like the myth of the Garden of Eden, such a view tends to see evil as outside, not within. It tends to see itself as perfect, as savior rather than sinner. It fails to warn people that there may be evil lurking behind its golden door.

There are several problems inherent in this situation. The first is the denial of power, especially the ambiguity of power and its use. Rollo May is strong on this point.

> The denial of our power, when it occurs in the endeavor to cover up an actually high degree of power, sets up an inner contradiction: power then does not allay our feelings of powerlessness. It does not lead to

the sense of responsibility that actual power ought to entail. We cannot develop responsibility for what we do not admit we have. We cannot act upon our power directly, for we always carry an element of guilt at having it. If we were to admit it, we would have to confront our guilt.[10]

The denial of power does not make power go away. To say, as Charles Reich does in *The Greening of America*, that "the very existence of power is an evil"[11] is to opt for an innocence that refuses to deal with the complexities at hand. To deny power ultimately is to deny one's own existence, and such impotence leads to violence.

Coupled with this denial of power in the pursuit of innocence is a denial of history, the second problem inherent in America's view of itself.

For history is the record, among other things, of man's sins and evils, of wars and the confrontations of power, and all the other manifestations of man's struggle toward an enlarged and deepened consciousness. Hence so many of the new generation turn their backs on history as irrelevant; they do not like it, they are not part of it, they insist we are in a brand new ball game with new rules. And they are completely unaware that this is the ultimate act of hubris.[12]

George Santayana once said that those who forget the past are doomed to repeat it.

The third problem is the denial of evil. This is the innocence that has blinders on, that refuses to take account of evil in order to avoid the complexity that the presence of evil entails. Involved here is the projection of evil which is a particular problem inherent in American society in regard to innocence.

It is the rather naive notion that the bad guy is always the other guy, that America is always in the right—in pursuit of true ideals and values. "My country right or wrong but my country" is laudable in regard to loyalty but lamentable in regard to honesty. The shift from loyalty to honesty is a very important watershed in moral sensitivity in the past twenty years. Both loyalty and honesty need to be held in tension if we are to avoid the blinders of a false innocence (in a preoccupation with loyalty) or harshness of distant judgment (in a preoccupation with honesty).

America must avoid the false innocence of seeing itself as the guardian of rights and freedom while failing to appreciate the evil from within. This clear-cut projection of evil has broken down in recent years, especially since the Vietnam debacle. On the other hand this sensitivity to evil within our own borders (which includes the evil inside ourselves—something not always appreciated) should not then blind us to the evil outside and leave us naive about evil forces around the world whether they be in the form of communism or terrorism. In failing to appreciate the complexities entailed we can be involved in complicity with evil or inadvertently contribute to a greater evil.

For the Christian believer there is another fundamental and important dimension that goes beyond tactics of how to handle evil. That is the very real and imperative challenge of the Gospel of Jesus Christ. Once you recognize evil as evil, then what do you do? Can you engage in evil in your attempt to conquer evil? What is the Christian challenge to love your enemies? Here is where our loyalties to being a Christian and being an American may part ways. It is one of the most crucial and personal questions we each face. It is the place where conversion occurs.

Fourth, Rollo May presents another form of pseudo-innocence that I find particularly intriguing. It has to do with the use of law and order. It is an expression of innocence first in its assumption that violence and aggression can be dealt with by force, and it assumes an identification between law and a particular order that happens to exist at that moment in society. "My" order therefore becomes "right" and even identified with the will of God. "Law coupled with order, in the shibboleth 'law and order,' becomes regularly a justification of the status quo. . . . Emphasis on law and order can be destructive to a person's self-esteem and self-respect."[13] An emphasis on law and order removes from the individual the responsibility that is proper to one living a human life. It places evil outside oneself—in the transgression of law and the disruption of order. It thereby fails to recognize evil for what it is and for where it truly lies. Evil is not some impersonal force, some quantifiable reality. Evil at its root is a personal reality. It is within and between people. An innocence that thinks that evil can be dealt with by force of law is a pseudo-innocence. Evil can only be dealt with when people recognize its presence and assume responsibility for it. Rosemary Haughton talks about transformation taking place in the gaps in our existence, when the law breaks down.[14] This transformation or conversion is possible when we recognize evil for what it is and desire to change.

Hiroshima, Vietnam, and Watergate have had lasting effects upon the consciousness of Americans. We have lost much of our pretense to innocence. Hopefully we are coming into a new maturity in our understanding of ourselves and our relationships with other nations.

The Cry for Significance

The basic arena in which powerlessness is an adversary of spirituality is in the arena of the human person. The cry for significance is the particularly painful cry of people today. If someone is not listening to us on the deepest level on which we live, we will be frustrated and lonely persons. And often it cannot be just anyone listening but someone who is significant in our lives. That deepest level touches the very basic level of our being: our feelings, convictions, hopes, and dreams. The cry for significance has taken us down some dead end paths: in the pursuit of power and prestige, in the accumulation of material goods, in the mad scramble for pleasure and recognition. It is the attempt to fill the hole at the center of the doughnut rather than to recognize and face a critical spiritual issue: that there is a gap in our existence that can only be met by addressing the spiritual transcendental dimension to our being. It is the paradox of powerlessness—on the one hand, a recognition of our worth, that we possess power in being who we are; on the other hand, a recognition of our incompleteness, a surrender of ourselves to the God who loves us. This is the recognition of St. Paul that in weakness power reaches perfection (2 Cor 12:10). In another vein Henri Nouwen speaks about this in terms of loneliness. He says that we are not called upon to take one another's loneliness away, that such is a divine expectation placed upon human beings. Rather, he says we need to face that loneliness and discover within it a solitude that is the beginning of a spiritual life, an openness to the transcendent.[15]

It is within this context of recognizing the need for us to face our own finiteness and look into our spirit to find meaning and strength that I would like to address the issue of powerlessness in the human person. I am not opting for a negative approach that sees us as nothing, as worthless. Rather, I am opting for a positive approach which recognizes that we are created in the image and likeness of God, and I would like to explore the meaning and value of our power in this regard. This cry for significance has three dimensions: self-affirmation, self-assertion, and self-expression. They are experienced as levels of need. They can become expressions of power when these needs are addressed and met.

1. The Need To Be Recognized: Self-Affirmation

We cannot just be told we are significant. We must discover it in our own lived experience. It is not enough to be a son or daughter of God; we need to discover the meaning of such a reality in our own life. The need to be recognized, self-affirmation, "arises from an original feeling of worth imparted to the infant through the love of a parent or parents in the early months and it shows itself later on in life in a sense of dignity."[16] This feeling of intrinsic worth is essential for every mentally healthy human being. The experience of powerlessness on this level is very crippling.

Conrad Baars and Anna Terruwe have developed the notion of deprivation neurosis to express the condition of powerlessness and pain that people experience in their emotionally impoverished history. In their book *Healing the Unaffirmed* they distinguish this type of neurosis from repression where certain feelings for a specific stage of life are prevented from developing by the mechanism of repression. The syndrome of a deprivation neurosis results from the frustration or deprivation of a natural sensitive need for affirmation in the infant, baby, or growing child by the mother, father, or both.[17] The powerlessness involved in a deprivation neurosis is reflected in the typical symptoms of lack of self-esteem, constant attempts to please others and defer to them, and childlike feelings of self-centeredness. This particular neurosis shows in dramatic ways the necessity of love and affection from others. The process of self-affirmation does not take place in a void but through interaction with others. For all of us life begins with total helplessness and dependence upon others not only physically but psychologically and emotionally as well.

One story from my childhood has always remained with me as an affirming experience. As a little boy I had even more freckles than I have now. I can remember feeling very self-conscious about them, not wanting to be different, afraid there was something wrong with me. My father told me they were Irish diamonds, that they were signs of God's love. I accepted that and it really made a difference; I not only lost my shame of freckles but I became proud of them. It was a simple enough explanation that strikes me as humorous yet no less true today. At the time it was a great grace. My father took the time to talk to me and, with his customary positive spirit, he helped me feel good about myself. As I think about it, the grace involved is not primarily a clever explanation. The grace goes deeper. It involves my father's love for me, my acceptance of myself, and the underlying peace that characterized our lives.

Unless we come to terms with this issue of self-affirmation we run the danger later on (as distinct from deprivation neurosis) of seizing upon power as a means of gaining recognition with others. Here power will be identified mainly with force and will be largely misused because it will be focused on a lack within ourselves, not on healthy interaction with others. In Chapter III we will return to this notion of self-affirmation in regard to the misconception that self-affirmation is a selfish or ego-centered concept. The notion that we must hate ourselves and depreciate ourselves is a spiritually vapid notion. Jesus told us to love our neighbor not as we hate ourselves but as we love ourselves. Love of self, self-acceptance, self-affirmation is a necessary prerequisite for loving another. Powerlessness, then, on this level, is an adversary of spirituality because it does not allow us to give of ourselves. We cannot give what we do not think we have to give. Healthy spiritual growth involves giving of ourselves. Giving of ourselves involves a recognition of who we are and what we have to give. This comes from interaction with others where we are recognized and affirmed as persons of worth and dignity. Thus, self-affirmation is a basic form of power. Self-assertion and self-expression are ways of living out our self-worth.

2. The Need To Be Respected: Self-Assertion

We do not live in the best of all worlds. Rather we live in a world where conflicts exist, where opposing forces come into play to determine action and events. Self-affirmation does not answer all the questions that power places before us. "When self-affirmation no longer works . . . the individual gathers his or her powers together to pit against the opposition."[18] In one's struggle between power and powerlessness there is not only the need to be recognized, there is also the need to be respected.

One of my previous superiors, whenever we disagreed about something, would always appeal to his authority, to his power, in order to end discussion: "I'm the boss here. We'll do things my way." To which I would reply, "I know that. But as long as I live here you will always know what I think." It was an exercise of power on my part. He was a nervous man, and as long as he knew what I thought he was not really free to just do things his way. My self-assertion was an exercise of power between us. It could only take place in the face of his opposition. If I simply resigned myself to my own powerlessness in the light of his authority (a form of power) I would have been frustrated and angry, and this in itself would have been a source of oppression or violence. Even if I did not change a given situation, the exercise of my self-assertion, of my power was very important to my own well-being. The fact that I did succeed in influencing decisions and effecting change (albeit occasionally) was important in my growing sense of myself and my own self-worth. Continual defeat at the hands of someone who rejected or destroyed my expressions of self-assertion might have corroded my sense of self-worth. However, in the given situation, even though I might not win a particular battle, I could at least walk away with my integrity intact knowing that by asserting myself and being true to my beliefs I had exercised my power as best I could.

3. The Need To Be Heard: Self-Expression

This is an inarticulate generation. Many people today do not know how to express themselves. This in itself is a source of much violence. The powerlessness of not being able to express oneself is another form of powerlessness that is an adversary of spirituality. It undercuts self-affirmation and self-assertion, for, if one cannot express oneself, one will quickly be frustrated in one's efforts at self-affirmation and self-assertion. Assuming that one is in touch with one's feelings (an assumption I would not quickly make), the ability to express oneself is very important in the exercise of one's power. In speaking of self-expression I am not talking about the ability to argue well, yell louder, or get in the last word. By self-expression I mean the basic ability to put words to what is happening inside oneself.

Sometimes people are not sure just how they feel or what is happening inside them until they attempt to express it. For some this takes the form of speaking, for others writing. Others may find expression in gestures or symbols. But the need for self-expression remains. Powerlessness at this level leads to violence. Billy Budd, in Herman Melville's novel *Billy Budd, Foretopman*, is a good example. At his trial after he had killed the master-at-arms with his fist, he exclaims, "Could I have used my tongue I would not have struck him. . . . I could only say it with a blow." Rollo May comments, "Not being able to find his tongue (because of his severe stuttering) he could only speak by means of the physical expression of his passion."[19]

III. Perspectives for Christian Living

Powerlessness and the Gospels

The Gospels are often interpreted as denouncing power in order to be a follower of Christ. It is presumed too quickly that power itself is evil and needs to be renounced in order for one to be a Christian. Is power itself incongruent with the Gospel? What do we do with power? What kind of power does Jesus espouse in inaugurating his kingdom? How is powerlessness an adversary of the Gospels? In the Beatitudes in Matthew 5, Jesus offers a blessing:

> How happy are the poor in spirit;
> theirs is the kingdom of heaven.
> Happy the gentle: they shall
> have the earth for their heritage. . . .
> Happy those who are persecuted in
> the cause of right: theirs is the
> kingdom of heaven (Mt 5:3–4. 10).

In Matthew 25 Jesus commends to his followers the least of his brethren:

> I tell you solemnly, insofar as
> you did this to one of the least

of these brothers of mine, you
did it to me. . . . Insofar as you neglected to do
this to one of the least of these,
you neglected to do it to me (Mt 25:40. 45).

Do what? "Feed the hungry, give drink to the thirsty, welcome
the stranger, visit those in prison." Jesus exercises power and
he hands that power on to his followers, "power from on high."
"Whoever believes in me will perform the same works as I do
myself; he will perform even greater works because I am going
to the Father" (Jn 14:12). Jesus offers a clear challenge to his
followers indicating a reversal of the order of the world: "For
anyone who wants to save his life will lose it; but anyone who
loses his life for my sake will find it. What, then, will a man gain
if he wins the whole world and ruins his life?" (Mt 16:25–26).
    Surely Jesus expresses deep concern for the poor and the
downtrodden in his ministry. His miracles bring healing to the
blind, the lame, and the deaf. His compassion brings forgiveness of sins to those who have gone astray. His preaching brings
comfort and hope to many. It is important to recognize that
these are forms of power. Miracles of healing, forgiveness of
sins, and preaching the word are exercises of power. In Chapter
2 of Mark's Gospel Jesus is confronted with a paralyzed man
whose friends have gone to great length to have him walk
again. To their surprise Jesus says to him, "My child, your sins
are forgiven" (Mk 2:5). This is an exercise of power that they
are not prepared for. They do not think Jesus has the right to
forgive sins nor do they particularly think this man needs it—
a curious combination of powerlessness and innocence. In
order to make this point about the power he has to forgive sins,
Jesus meets them on their own terms with an exercise of power:
"I order you, get up, pick up your stretcher and go off home"
(Mk 2:12). But he also makes it clear that the more important
power is the forgiveness of sins.

Power is a given: it is an inevitable reality in the world in which we live. Power itself is not evil. The use of certain forms of power or the abuse of power is where several questions arise. Exploitative and manipulative power are forms of power that are incongruent with the Gospel because they are power over others. Nutrient and integrative power are congruent with the Gospel precisely because they are forms of power at the service of others. The power which Jesus exercises is not power as the world uses it, just as the peace which Jesus gives is a peace that the world cannot give. Thus power is congruent with the Gospels. I think it is the height of pseudo-innocence to use the Gospels as an argument against power itself, to posit that power itself is evil, and to believe that one is not using power in one's dealings with others. It is a more authentic Gospel response to discover the Christian meaning of power and how to use it at the service of others.

It is also healthy from a psychological point of view. Holiness and wholeness, while not co-extensive or synonymous, are meant to work in harmony with each other. In other words, spiritual development and human growth go hand in hand in the development of a healthy human being. This does not mean that a person must be "together" psychologically in order to grow spiritually. Nor does it mean that spiritual growth can ignore psychological factors in the development of the human person. But it does mean that the integration of the two is the goal in the development of mature healthy human beings. Powerlessness is an obstacle to both spiritual growth and psychological health. Self-affirmation, self-assertion, and self-expression are fundamental to the issue of power in regard to one's sense of oneself. As people of faith, as followers of Jesus Christ, denial of self does not mean the negation of oneself but the discovery of one's true identity in Christ. This means a recognition of who one is and how one can authentically live one's own identity as a son or daughter of God.

St. Paul expresses this well in his writings. In the Epistle to the Ephesians he prays for the people: "This, then, is what I pray, kneeling before the Father, from whom every family, whether spiritual or natural, takes its name: Out of his infinite glory, may he give you the power through his Spirit for your hidden self to grow strong, so that Christ may live in your hearts through faith" (Eph 3:14–17). This is not the negation of power. It is the recognition of the meaning of power in relationship to love and faith. "Then, planted in love and built on love, you will with all the saints have strength to grasp the breadth and the length, the height and the depth; until, knowing the love of Christ, which is beyond all knowledge, you are filled with the utter fullness of God" (Eph 3:17–19).

When Paul says that it is in weakness that power reaches perfection (2 Cor 12:10), he is not espousing powerlessness as a condition of the Gospels. He is rather describing a power different from the world's use of authority and force. He is encouraging us to find our strength in Christ and in the power of love which flows from a deep sense of ourselves as spiritual beings. Paul illustrates this by talking about a "thorn in his flesh," a weakness or fault that Paul prayed would be taken away. It became an opportunity for him to touch the real source of his power as a man of faith:

> About this thing, I have pleaded with the Lord three times for it to leave me, but he has said, "My grace is enough for you; my power is at its best in weakness." So I shall be very happy to make my weaknesses my special boast so that the power of Christ may stay over me, and that is why I am quite content with my weaknesses, and with insults, hardships, persecutions, and the agonies I go through for Christ's sake. For it is when I am weak that I am strong (2 Cor 12:8–10).

Paul sees our pride as an obstacle to God's power working within us. He sees our true strength, our true dignity to be found in our spiritual dimension, in our transcendence into the presence of God. "It was to shame the wise that God chose what is foolish by human reckoning, and to shame what is strong that he chose what is weak by human reckoning; those whom the world thinks common and contemptible are the ones that God has chosen—those who are nothing at all to show up those who are everything. . . . If anyone wants to boast, let him boast about the Lord" (1 Cor 1:27–31). Paul testifies to his own experience in this regard:

> As for me, brothers, when I came to you, it was not with any show of oratory or philosophy, but simply to tell you what God has guaranteed. During my stay with you, the only knowledge I claimed to have was about Jesus, and only about him as the crucified Christ. Far from relying on any power of my own, I came among you in great "fear and trembling," and in my speeches and the sermons that I gave, there were none of the arguments that belong to philosophy, only a demonstration of the power of the Spirit. And I did this so that your faith should not depend on human philosophy but on the power of God (1 Cor 2:1–5).

The fundamental point about power and the Gospels is the paradox of the cross of Christ which Paul referred to in the preceding passage. On the cross Christ subjects himself to the power of men—a power over his very life. In that act of giving and surrender he effected the in-breaking of a greater power— the power of love, a healing and life-giving power to a broken world.

Innocence and the Gospels

The Gospels are also interpreted in favor of an innocence that is naive and that is kept safe from the realities of evil and sin. Innocence can be used as a flight from that responsibility that is ours in the struggle of good and evil. That struggle exists both within us and around us. How does innocence which puts on blinders work as an adversary of spirituality? What does it mean to be as cunning as serpents and as gentle as doves? What is authentic innocence in spiritual growth?

Again, in the Beatitudes Jesus offers a blessing:

> Happy the pure in heart; they shall see God. Happy the peacemakers; they shall be called sons of God (Mt 5:8–9).

Purity of heart means not having mixed emotions. It implies that one has recognized one's own evil and faced it while relying on the power of God's love. A person who is innocent, in the sense of naive, unaware, is more likely, rather than less likely, to have mixed emotions because he or she just doesn't know what all the motives operating within himself or herself are. Such innocence which implies a lack of knowledge is an adversary of spirituality especially because God is all-knowing.

In Matthew, Mark, and Luke, Jesus presents little children as the example of those who will enter the kingdom of God. "Let the little children come to me; do not stop them; for it is to such as these that the kingdom of God belongs. I tell you solemnly, anyone who does not welcome the kingdom of God like a little child will never enter it" (Mk 10:14–15). What exactly does this mean? What is Jesus recommending to us? I suppose this depends upon one's image of little children. If one sees little children as pure and "innocent," then one may deduce that

Jesus is recommending to us that we must be naive and unaware of evil in order to enter the kingdom of God. If one sees little children as selfish monsters, then one may go to the other extreme and deduce that Jesus is recommending that we think only of ourselves in order to enter the kingdom of God. In using children as an example I do not think that Jesus is recommending the innocence of naiveté nor is he discarding innocence as a quality of the kingdom. I think he is recommending the trust and honesty of children that both recognizes goodness (trust) and sees evil for what it really is (honesty).

Authentic innocence does not exclude a knowledge and awareness of evil. Authentic innocence involves a choice for the good in the face of temptation toward evil, not in the absence of such a temptation. When Jesus commends the pure in heart he is commending those who have struggled with and internalized the Gospel values which Jesus has given us and have remained faithful to them.

There are people who are especially gifted by the Lord with a positive Christian spirit. Nathanael, described in the first chapter of John's Gospel as a man without guile, is a good example. "When Jesus saw Nathanael coming he said of him, 'There is an Israelite who deserves the name, incapable of deceit'" (Jn 1:48). This form of innocence is a natural quality some people possess, a quality of their spirit which is a real gift. They bear a burden for this gift in coming to terms with the reality of evil, as we shall see in the case of Billy Budd.

Innocence then, to be authentic, must be a true expression of a person's spirit and character. It cannot be a flight from reality or an abdication of responsibility. It must be the result of one's struggle between good and evil both within oneself and around oneself. That struggle, its nature and characteristics, will differ from person to person. Some people have a more naturally positive and open disposition than others. Some will find the struggle with evil to be a deep struggle within themselves.

Others will find that struggle in coming to terms with the evil they encounter around them. An innocence that puts blinders on evil within or without is an innocence which is an adversary of spirituality.

When I was first ordained and working in a parish, there were many challenges before me that called for adjustment and reconciliation. There were the challenges referred to earlier of listening to people tell their stories of brokenness and fear. There were the many activities and programs that filled each week and each passing season. There were the adjustments to a new lifestyle: living in a rectory, living and working in the same place, encountering differences in conviction and approach. I found myself being very inconsistent that first year. There were days when I was running around from one project to another enthusiastic about the new things I was doing. On such days I hardly noticed those with whom I was living and working. On other days, in my idealism, I was expecting everyone to be as energetic and enthusiastic as I thought I was.

After a while I began to realize that this revealed a deep inconsistency in me. It became symbolized through a talk our seminary rector had given the year before where he spoke about expectations in terms of whether the cup was half empty or half full. On the days when I was preoccupied with my own work I thought the cup was half empty and expected little of others. But, when things were slow or life was frustrating, I looked out with all my idealism and, thinking the cup was half full, expected others to measure up to my standards.

Coming to terms with this was an important conversion that year. Others were being consistent and probably could not figure out my moods and vacillation. Whatever the reality of persons and events around me, I had to accept them as they were and then face the Christian challenge before me: seeing people and situations as they were with all their limitations and failings, now the challenge of being a Christian was all the more real and personal. As long as I was trying to fashion reality to my own liking, I could pick and choose the ways in which I would love. As long as I put on blinders to evil or projected it on to others, I would continue along my own narrow way. But precisely the conversion that marked those days was to see people and situations in all their reality (positive and negative) and then respond with integrity and love.

Power and Love: Compassion

In developing a spirituality which takes account of powerlessness and innocence, it will be most helpful to examine the relationship between power and love. Traditionally love and power have been viewed as opposites: the more power one shows, the less love; the more love, the less power. "Love is seen as powerless and power as loveless."[1] I heartily agree with Rollo May when he attacks this dichotomy as a misunderstanding of both power and love. I think that dichotomizing power and love is one of the foundations of powerlessness and innocence as adversaries of spirituality.

To say that one can love and renounce power is to fall into the trap of pseudo-innocence because it fails to take account of the realistic difficulties of love and the inevitable struggle between good and evil which love itself entails. As a matter of fact one cannot love unless one recognizes that one has power. 'Ya can't give what ya don't got.' Rollo May expresses this a little more conventionally: "That power and love are interrelated is proved most of all by the fact that one must have power within oneself in order to love in the first place. . . . A person must have something to give in order not to be completely taken over or absorbed as a nonentity."[2] Involved here is a misunderstanding of both power and love. "The fallacy of this juxtaposition of love and power comes from our seeing love purely as an emotion and power solely as force of compulsion. We need to understand them both as ontological, as states of being or processes."[3]

Basic human insecurity is at the root of much of the difficulty here in the dichotomy of love and power. An insecure person does not have less to offer; rather he does not offer what he has. When people are not secure within themselves they tend to latch on to power as force and will use forms of power (exploitative and manipulative power) that have a low relationship to love. They will try to make up for a lack within themselves. Love will suffer equally as well, being turned into a mere emotion. When people are not secure within themselves (not a static reality but itself a process) they will cling to others in possessiveness rather than give to others in love.

Surely love involves a reciprocity in giving and receiving in which people grow in their sense of themselves and come to know themselves and believe in themselves in the process of loving and being loved. But if they are not grounded somewhere, love will go nowhere. The process of spiritual, personal growth involves peeling off the layers of the false self, sifting through these layers of insecurity to reach the core of one's identity. As people begin to appreciate that, at the heart of who they are as spirit, is the creative love of God for them, they can begin to peel off these layers of the false self. The process begins not with a focus on insecurity nor even with the focus on the self. The process of the spiritual life begins with a focus on God's love and his action in our lives here and now. Then love and power can come together in strength. Love and power need to be seen in a dialectical relationship if they are to be at the service of spiritual growth.

We must turn our attention to the interplay between love and power, and the fact that love needs power if it is to be more than sentimentality and that power needs love if it is not to slip into manipulation. Power without charity ends up in cruelty. The constructive forms of power, such as nutrient power and integrative power, come only when there has already been built within the individual some self-esteem and self-affirmation.[4]

While giving a retreat several years ago I met a man who told me the beautiful story of his journey that amounted to the integration of power and love. Jack was about forty-two at the time of our conversation. He had grown up in a very loving family and had many opportunities before him. As a teenager he found out by accident something his parents had kept from him for a long time: he was adopted as an infant. At first this did not bother him though it came as a shock. However, being in the throes of the search for identity and the struggle for self-possession as an adolescent, he found himself haunted by this gap in his life. Who was he? Who were his original parents? Why did they give him up? "Was I given up out of love or out of hate?" was a question that became a central focus for him. There were no available answers and, at any rate, he kept most of these questions bottled up inside himself. The only parents he knew obviously loved him and cared deeply for him. So these questions only caused further conflict and guilt in the feeling of betraying them by even asking such questions. He felt helpless and unworthy of love, confused and afraid.

He was unable to appreciate the larger picture. People told him that his original parents probably were victims of circumstances themselves and may have been very courageous in giving him to people who could care for him. They pointed out that the parents he knew had chosen him freely and did love him deeply. But, that gap, that uncertainty, became a cancer that grew and grew. He married a woman who had not experienced much love or affection in her family and who made up for her insecurities through the use of power as force over people. As they began raising a family of their own, Jack was firmly on a road of disintegration. His sense of humor and cheerful spirit began to fade and was replaced by a facade to keep people away. Lacking a sense of himself, he was prey to every comment or derision that came his way. Before long alcohol and pills were draining his life and sapping his strength. Anyone who tried to reach out to him was politely rebuffed. His wife was forbearing but was caught in a prison of her own.

I listened to his story wondering how he ever came to be sitting in front of me so calm and together. As it turned out his was one of those stories that leaves one in awe at the presence of grace. He simply looked at himself in the mirror one morning and admitted he had a problem and needed help. He looked up "Alcoholics Anonymous" in the telephone book and went to a meeting that day and each day thereafter for three months. Gradually he began to accept himself and come to terms with his past. The support and love of his own family and his AA family enabled him to gain new strength and come to a healthy sense of himself. I have the greatest respect for recovered alcoholics because they have the courage to face each day, one at a time. They are people who have harmonized power and love in a realistic and humble sense of themselves that explodes with compassion.

Compassion ties power and love together and is, in my opinion, one of the most important qualities of spirituality today. Compassion, when love and power are viewed as opposites, is often seen as a weak, wishy-washy form of love. But if compassion is understood properly as the interplay of power and love it is a fundamental link between people. Rollo May holds that the development of power is a prerequisite for compassion: "Compassion requires that one have some security, some position of power from which he can give concern to another."[5] Once again he links a healthy sense of oneself (the opposite of powerlessness) with one's ability to love. "Lack of

self-esteem and self-affirmation makes it difficult to have anything left over with which to 'prime the pump' before he can
give to others."[6]

Compassion links us to one another. In compassion nothing
is alien to us. Thomas Merton once thanked God that he was
like the rest of men. Says Rollo May:

> Compassion is the name of that form of love which is
> based on our knowing and understanding each other.
> Compassion is the awareness that we are all in the
> same boat and that we all shall either sink or swim
> together. Compassion arises from the recognition of
> community. . . . Compassion gives us a basis for arriv-
> ing at the humanistic position which will include both
> power and love. Compassion occupies a position oppo-
> site to violence; as violence projects hostile images of
> the opponent, compassion accepts such daimonic
> impulses in one's self. It gives us the basis for judging
> someone without condemning him. Although loving
> one's enemies requires grace, compassion for one's
> enemies is a human possibility.[7]

There is no room for pseudo-innocence in compassion
because compassion not only recognizes evil but recognizes
one's own capacity for evil. In such a situation, the starting
point for spirituality is not a linear path upward untouched by
the presence of evil and sin. The starting point is rather a recognition of our common humanity, of our common struggle to
deal with evil not as something outside ourselves but as something we are familiar with.

The Daimonic

This leads us naturally into some reflections on the daimonic. We have already seen that innocence which cannot

include the daimonic becomes evil. So the first point about the daimonic is that we must recognize its presence and develop an appreciation of its influence in our lives for creativity as well as for aggression. Sheldon Kopp (in his book *If You Meet the Buddha on the Road, Kill Him*) writes: "No one can afford to give up any part of himself. All of you is worth something. Even the evil can be a source of vitality if only you can face it and transform it."[8] Notice the dynamic which takes place in war. "At the outset of every war we hastily transform our enemy into the image of the daimonic, and then, since it is the devil we are fighting, we can shift onto a war footing without asking ourselves all the troublesome psychological and spiritual questions that the war arouses. We no longer have to face the realization that those we are killing are persons like ourselves."[9]

In recognizing the presence of the daimonic we have to recognize its presence within, not merely without. As a matter of fact, the projection of the daimonic onto others is a common way of not only avoiding the daimonic within but also of justifying the evil we do to others. Our capacity for evil hinges upon our breaking through our pseudo-innocence and owning the daimonic as we encounter it in others and in ourselves. Once again Rollo May sums this up well:

> It is a considerable boon for a person to realize that he has his negative side like everyone else, that the daimonic works in potentiality for both good and evil, and that he can neither disown it nor live without it. It is similarly beneficial when he also comes to see that much of his achievement is bound up with the very conflicts this daimonic impulse engenders. This is the seal of the experience that life is a mixture of good and evil; that there is no such thing as pure good; and that if the evil weren't there as a potentiality, the good

would not be either. Life consists of achieving good not apart from evil but in spite of it.[10]

Carl Jung has some very instructive thoughts on this when he talks about the shadow. He locates the shadow in the personal unconscious: "To become conscious of it involves reorganizing the dark aspects of the personality as present and real. This act is the essential condition for any kind of self-knowledge, and it therefore, as a rule, meets with considerable resistance."[11]

The dark characteristics of the shadow, the inferiorities constituting the shadow, possess an emotional nature, a kind of autonomy. Generally we project the more resistant aspects of the shadow onto other people. Since this is done unconsciously, one can be said to encounter projections, not manufacture them. All of this makes the owning of one's shadow no easy task and helps explain the difficulty many people face in coming to terms with their capacity for evil. It should also be pointed out that Jung does not see the shadow as merely or primarily negative.

What our age thinks of as the inferior and shadow part of the psyche contains more than something merely negative. The very fact that through self-knowledge, i.e., by exploring our own souls, we come upon the instincts and their world of imagery should throw some light on the powers slumbering in the psyche, of which we are seldom aware so long as everything goes well. They are potentialities of the greatest dynamism and it depends entirely upon the preparedness and attitude of the conscious mind whether the irruption of these forces and the images and ideas associated with them will tend toward construction or catastrophe.[12]

Jung's description of the shadow and its simultaneously dark and dynamic potentialities leading to either catastrophe or destruction sheds light on the notion of the daimonic as Rollo May develops it. Rollo May uses "daimonic" where we might expect "demonic." He is using the notion of daimonic to include evil not just in terms of evil as force or spirit but as potentiality for creativity and dynamism.

Billy Budd and Claggart in Herman Melville's novel *Billy Budd, Foretopman* both provide rich examples of the implications of the daimonic in life. Billy Budd is pictured as the personification of innocence. Apparently he is loved by everyone. He has a sunny disposition and is a strong and attractive person. But he totters on the edge of being too good to be true. He has one physical difficulty which proves to be symbolic: he stutters when his emotions are aroused. Claggart, on the other hand, is much more schooled in the ways of the world and much more astute about the presence of the daimonic in life. He is both attracted and repelled by Billy Budd's innocence. The daimonic had hold of Claggart and would make him its victim. He apprehended the good but was powerless to be so and consequently resented anyone who embodied the goodness which eluded his grasp.

Billy and Claggart are a match for each other. Their respective tragic flaws meet in such a way that tragedy is inevitable. Billy is approached by a shipmate to plan a mutiny. He stoutly refuses but does not want to hurt the shipmate's feelings and would not think of turning him in. He refuses to see evil as evil. Claggart denounces Billy as mutineer and Billy is called to defend himself. Claggart is driven to destroy the innocence he cannot abide and Billy is oblivious to the daimonic which threatens his innocence. In his defense Billy becomes frustrated by his stuttering and in his powerless rage he kills Claggart with a single blow. Billy goes to the gallows with his innocence intact proclaiming a blessing on Captain Vere.

Billy is an admirable and yet tragic figure. Why did he not sense Claggart's enmity toward him? He had been warned many times that Claggart did not like him, that he was out to "get" him. But Billy kept finding a positive interpretation to preserve his perspective on total goodness. As Melville himself says, "Innocence was his blinder."[13] There must have been some need in Billy not to see. He benefits from his own strategy, intentionally or not. He wants to be liked and to get ahead and his innocence provides him with the means to those ends. In Billy's case, spirituality is opposed to innocence.

> All of this adds up to the fact that Billy is innocent but not spiritual. For the latter requires and is based upon experience—it tempers the self, deepens consciousness and awareness, purges and sharpens our sight, as Melville says—whereas innocence acts as a blinder and tends to keep us from growing, from new awareness, from identifying with the sufferings of mankind as well as its joys (both being foreign to the innocent person). These are two potential poles of experience: to remain innocent, blocking out what does not appeal to you, striving to preserve the Garden of Eden state; or to strive toward spirituality and move to the "deeper music of humanity," in Wordsworth's phrase.[14]

Finally Rollo May raises an interesting question which he later answers concerning Billy Budd: "Does the victim have something to do with making himself the victim?"[15] His answer is affirmative:

> The real tragic flaw in Billy Budd can now be stated: he blocked off his own awareness of the effect he was having on Claggart despite the endeavors of the old sailor, Dansker, to point out Claggart's growing hostil-

ity toward him. Billy sought to preserve his own innocence. Indeed, his innocence was precisely the defense
against this crucial awareness—it was a shield behind
which he nursed his own childlikeness. His awareness
made the killing of Claggart and his own hanging
inevitable.[16]

There are two dimensions to Billy's blindness that deserve
further reflection. He was blind to the hostility Claggart har-
bored against him and he was blind to his own effect upon Claggart. He had a vested interest in both these dimensions. Billy's
childlike way worked for him. Surely, his childlikeness was
genuine. His spirit was graced with a guileless quality. To that
extent, Billy's innocence was spiritually sound. But, again, in
this broken world of ours goodness is fragile and evil is all too
real. Billy's innocence became a way of dealing with life and of
fashioning reality to his own advantage. If he did not admit
Claggart's evil intention he did not have to deal with it and, consequently, he did not have to face within himself the effect his
innocence had upon this man. Billy's innocence only made
Claggart more furious. While this is to a large extent Claggart's
problem, it is, nevertheless, a real problem. Billy needs to take
responsibility for his own innocence. The solution is not that
Billy should give up his childlike spirit. That would be to deny
something real and good about himself and such a denial would
lead to his own destruction. The challenge is for Billy to take
responsibility for this gift of his spirit in the real world that sur-
rounds him. This responsibility involves an ability to assess how
his innocence serves him well and how it serves him ill. It also
involves a greater awareness of his own vested interest in his
innocence.

IV. Some Contemporary Contributions

In this section I intend to present some ideas which contribute to the notion that powerlessness and innocence are adversaries of spirituality. It is my conviction that spirituality encompasses us as body and soul, mind and spirit. The search for living an authentic spiritual life takes place within a world that is incomplete and, indeed, broken. We cannot ignore evil and expect that it will not have its influence upon us. We cannot ignore the reality of power and abdicate our proper responsibility in regard to power. At the same time we must recognize that "spirituality is attention to the life of the spirit in us."[1] It is a recognition of self-transcendence and openness to the Spirit of God. The contributions that follow will help to shed light on the meaning of spirituality and the place of power and innocence.

Viktor Frankl: The Power of Meaning

Carl Jung once said: "About a third of my cases are suffering from no clinically definable neurosis but from the senselessness and emptiness of their lives. It seems to me, however, that this can be described as the general neurosis of our time."[2] I think this senselessness and emptiness are also the prime examples of the powerlessness which people experience in their lives and which are adversaries of spirituality. I have tried to show that being itself contains power—that I have power simply by existence. Here I intend to expand on this by looking at being, existence, as containing meaning which is the primary source of power for us.

In *Man's Search for Meaning*, Viktor Frankl presents a very graphic and reflective account of his experience of concentration camps during the Second World War. In one sense his is a dramatic account of powerlessness. Human beings were reduced to mere flesh and bones; they were deprived of every material possession; they were forced to labor and live in deplorable conditions; they were enslaved and tortured physically and mentally in a situation which often seemed hopeless. Many died in gas chambers or from disease in the camps. Others committed suicide. Some turned against their fellow inmates and manipulated their way into positions of authority. Those who survived had to come to terms in some way with the meaning of life. Somehow they had to develop or preserve an attitude toward their experience and themselves that enabled them to go on, to want to live even under these miserable and hopeless conditions.

Viktor Frankl presents this will to live in terms of the search for meaning which confronted all of them in their experience. He is fond of quoting Nietzsche: "He who has a *why* to live can bear with almost any *how*." I think that Frankl's presentation of meaning in existence is a form of power that is basic to a spiritual life and so I have entitled this section "The Power of Meaning." I find that the experience of meaninglessness and emptiness is common among people in our contemporary society. It is often a result of having discovered the transitoriness and emptiness of forms of power in which they have invested themselves, whether those forms are power as force, prestige, money, or position. It is also true that the frustrated will to meaning is compensated for by a will to power. Here again we see that the experience of powerlessness can be an adversary of spirituality. Powerlessness in the form of meaninglessness and emptiness can lead people to grasp at power in forms that do not lead to spiritual growth but to self-indulgence.

In searching out his experience Frankl talks about three phases in the mental reaction to camp life: the initial entry, the duration of captivity, and the period following his release and liberation. The first is characterized by shock when one's whole former life is taken away. The dehumanization and powerlessness involved in this process is staggering. Trying to cope in such a situation leads to the second phase—that of apathy, a kind of emotional death. Frankl describes this early adjustment as a struggle of longing for one's home and family and a disgust at all the ugliness around him. He points out that an abnormal reaction to an abnormal situation is normal behavior.[3] Thus initial shock gives way to a certain numbness and disgust to a certain deadness. Instead of turning away from the horrors and the beatings, the inmates would watch the atrocities before them.

However, Frankl points out that despite the degrading insults and dehumanization, it was possible for a spiritual life to deepen. "Sensitive people who were used to a rich intellectual life may have suffered much pain . . . but the damage to their inner selves was less. They were able to retreat from their terrible surroundings to a life of inner riches and spiritual freedom."[4] Here is where the power of meaning and the meaning of power begins to come to light. Even in circumstances where people were totally devoid of external power over their life they still had the possibility of exercising a power of their inner spirit that not only is not an adversary of spirituality but is a source of it. Powerlessness on this level would spell death, and those who committed suicide did so precisely because of the powerlessness they experienced within themselves in giving up hope and losing all meaning in their lives. The most beautiful expression of the prisoners' spiritual power and meaning is found in their concern for and dialogue with absent loved ones. Frankl's dialogue with his wife was a source of great freedom and encouragement to him. He could find meaning in his suffering because of his love for his wife. He was able, in given moments, to transcend his hopeless, meaningless world and give a resounding "yes" to his question of the existence of an ultimate purpose of life.

From his experience in concentration camps, it is Frankl's conviction that people's inner strength can rise above their outward fate, that they can preserve a vestige of spiritual freedom even in such terrible conditions of psychic and physical stress. The meaning people discovered which enabled them to want to live was a meaning which called them out of themselves—to be there for a child (who might not have been living) or to complete a scientific project. The power of meaning, then, involves a self-transcendence, a passing beyond oneself in giving oneself away or a deepening of one's spirit by an openness to a transcendent Spirit beyond. Here again, we meet the paradox of power and powerlessness. One has to go beyond oneself to find oneself; one has to let go in order to find.

The third phase of one's mental reaction involved the adjustment to release and liberation. Frankl describes this as a gradual coming to light of feelings of joy and freedom which had been buried in the long process of depersonalization that the prisoners had endured. The will to meaning which had kept a person going in the concentration camp would possibly now be challenged. "Woe to him who found that the person whose memory alone had given him courage in camp did not exist any more."[5] Surely such disillusionment can be crushing. Frankl does not seem really to answer what happens or can happen at this point. In his explanation of logo-therapy he does point out that meaning is personal to each individual and time-bound in that it is meaning for a given time. Perhaps it is enough that such meaning gave the prisoner the power to live at the time of desperation.

I think the search for meaning as Frankl presents it is an important dimension to living a spiritual life. What he talks about as an "existential vacuum" in the emptiness and boredom of people's lives is, I think, a fundamental obstacle to spirituality for contemporary men and women. Powerlessness is an adversary of spirituality when powerlessness is a negation of our own being and the meaning of our existence. In meaning there is power, and in the power of meaning there is a spiritual life.

Henri Nouwen: The Wounded Healer and The Hospitable Host

Henri Nouwen is an articulate spokesman on many issues which are of interest to Christian leaders. I would like to draw upon his expertise by looking at two images appropriate for thinking people facing powerlessness and innocence. These two images—the wounded healer and the hospitable host—are interrelated ways of dealing with the powerlessness and innocence of our time.

Nouwen describes contemporary man as nuclear man— man who lives in an age when instant destruction is possible. "Nuclear man is a man who has lost naive faith in the possibilities of technology and is painfully aware that the same powers that enable man to create new life-styles carry the potential for self-destruction."[6] In an age when nuclear destruction is a present danger people have lost faith in the past and in the future. They are dislocated in that they feel there has been a real break in the continuity of history because of the presence of such all-pervasive destruction as nuclear power; they live only for the "now" because they have lost hope in a meaningful future. Such powerlessness is a source of great pain for many people. The situation is further complicated by the fact that not everyone has the same reaction to nuclear destruction. While some see it as imminent danger, others do not see it as a real danger at all but as a means of self-defense. The Christian leader is called upon to minister in this context.

In developing his notion of the wounded healer Nouwen offers three characteristics of what he calls "tomorrow's leader" that I think are very appropriate. The first is the articulator of inner events. Perhaps the deepest source of loneliness and alienation for people today is the dislocation within. There is great confusion inside people today—a confusion of identity (who am I?), a confusion of emotions (people are out of touch with their own feelings), a confusion of direction (they are not sure what they want out of life) and, fundamentally, a confusion of meaning. Tomorrow's leader as the articulator of inner events is not someone who tells other people how they feel or what they should do. As such a leader I am, rather, someone who is attempting to articulate my own inner events and thus offer myself to others as a service of clarification. Such articulation does not lead to new revelations for others but to new light cast on their unarticulated experience. "You say what I suspected. You express what I vaguely felt." I cannot lead others out of the desert unless I have been there myself. I cannot offer hope if that hope does not come out of my own struggle with the confusion within me. I cannot heal the wounds of others until I am willing to recognize and bind up my own. This leads to the second characteristic of tomorrow's leader—compassion.

I regard compassion as a most important quality of the spiritual life and as the key conversion process in my life. Compassion puts me in touch with all people because compassion is a great equalizer. Compassion opens within me not only my own wounds but also my own evil. In compassion nothing is foreign to me. In compassion the schizophrenic, the phobic, the obsessive compulsive are not terms in a textbook or labels on an individual; in compassion they are in me in some way or other, in one degree or another. In compassion the murderer is not a mystery to me but touches some of my own anger and despair. This is both painful and frightening and it therefore requires courage to be a compassionate person. Nouwen speaks about this with clarity:

> Through compassion it is possible to recognize that the craving for love that men feel resides also in our own hearts, that the cruelty that the world knows all too well is also rooted in our own impulses. Through compassion we also sense our hope for forgiveness in our friends' eye and our hatred in their bitter mouths. When they kill, we know that we could have done it; when they give life we know that we can do the same. For a compassionate man nothing human is alien: no joy and no sorrow, no way of living and no way of dying.[7]

Compassion is the opposite of powerlessness and innocence which are adversaries of spirituality. Compassion contains power not as a force over others but as a source of understanding and strength. Compassion also contains an awareness of evil not as a projection outside myself but as a reality within. Therefore, compassion leads to community, to seeing my neighbor as one with me. Compassion is the ability to hold as one both the ideals I believe in and the people I love.

The third characteristic—contemplation—becomes essential if compassion is to lead to growth and not an excuse for the status quo. Contemplation is the ability to see and reflect, to name reality for what it is, to appreciate the hidden meaning of people and events. Just as the physical sense of sight needs distance, so does contemplation. But this is not the distance of non-involvement or isolation. It is not a distance which requires a flight from life. It is rather a distance which is the counterpoint of involvement. Both are necessary. It is the combination of compassion and contemplation which provides a proper balance for the Christian leader to be effective.

I believe that there is a contemplative dimension to each of us that our society and culture inhibits (and even, at times, prohibits) us from developing. We live in a world of activity and noise; we live in a society which applauds achievements and results, a society which worships power in the form of force, wealth, prestige. Because of this, the more humanizing and spiritualizing forms of power found in compassion and contemplation are relegated to the shadow. "The contemplative is someone who sees things for what they really are, who sees the real connections, who knows—as Thomas Merton used to say—'what the scoop is.'"[8] Contemplation is a stance toward life involving silence and reflection which enables people to appreciate the quality of mystery in life, to touch the depths of their own mystery, and to begin to make choices and decisions which flow from deeper sources within them.

People will vary in their ability to exercise this contemplative power. Developing the quality of silence in one's life is the best way to develop this contemplative dimension. By silence I don't mean the mere absence of words or cessation of activity. By silence I mean a quality of presence to myself and to others, especially to God. Silence allows us the space and the opportunity to quiet down the many noises within us and around us so that we may truly listen. What we hear will not always be that welcome or easy to hear. Therefore we have to have the courage to persevere in silence. After a while our own demons and fantasies will stop knocking on our door and we continue to listen now with a more rested spirit. We will hear the Lord in the gentle breeze and we will experience contemplation.

Then we will be able to offer hospitality to others. But before we can offer hospitality to others we need to be at home within ourselves. This involves being in touch with our capacity for evil as well as our capacity for good. It means facing our own loneliness and allowing it to give way to solitude. Nouwen talks about hospitality as "friendship for the guest" and "the freedom of the guest." Hospitality requires the creation of space within where others can come to gain a hearing and find a rest. "Hospitality, therefore, means primarily the creation of a free space where the stranger can enter and become a friend instead of an enemy. Hospitality is not to change people, but to offer them space where change can take place."[9] "The minister who has come to terms with his own loneliness and is at home in his own house is a host who offers hospitality to his guests. He gives them friendly space, where they may feel free to come and go, to be close and distant, to rest and to play, to talk and to be silent, to eat and to fast."[10]

Accomplishing this means wrestling with one's own powerlessness and innocence, for these can be obstacles to creating free and empty space for others. Powerlessness becomes an adversary not only of spirituality but also of ministry when one does not tap the sources of power within oneself (especially compassion and contemplation) which can enable one to be a wounded healer who brings hope and encouragement to others. Innocence becomes an adversary not only of spirituality but also of ministry when one does not recognize the forces of evil which clutter one's mind and heart and thus prevent one from offering free space to a guest.

Powerlessness and innocence are obstacles to compassion and hospitality because they leave a void rather than free space, they alienate rather than welcome the guest in all his or her humanness. To be a wounded healer and a hospitable host one must first have come to know and take responsibility for one's potential for good and for evil. As one struggles toward this goal of wholeness and integrity oneself, one will be a valuable traveling companion for others who come to tell their story and share their journey.

John Paul II: The Concept of Mercy

In 1980 John Paul II issued an encyclical on the mercy of God. I intend to use his reflection on mercy to examine further the true meaning of power and authentic innocence in spiritual growth. It is not that power in itself is evil, but that power, as it is used by the worldly and greedy, can be a source of oppression for people. Power must be more clearly defined. Christ used power to move hearts and to heal them. But his power was the power of love and mercy. Powerlessness is an adversary of spirituality not because it is ineffective in human relationships and social structures. Powerlessness is an adversary of spirituality because it denies the truth of ourselves as worthwhile and good. We must recognize the power we have if we are to live authentic human and spiritual lives, and we must recognize the source of that power in the love and mercy of God. One of the functions of the Christian leader is to help people make connections in their lives between their human burdens and crosses and the cross of Christ, between their efforts to love and the love God first has for them. It is the challenge of the Christian leader to help bring their faith to bear on their human struggles and shed light upon their human drama.

John Paul builds this encyclical *On the Mercy of God* upon his first encyclical *Redemptor Hominis,* in which he emphasized and upheld the dignity of the human person. In discussing both powerlessness and innocence it is important to remember that we are created good, not evil. It has been my premise that innocence is an adversary of spirituality when it fails to take account of evil. But it must be emphasized that we at root are not evil but good, created in the image and likeness of God. "God saw all he had made, and indeed it was very good" (Gn 1:31). Herein lies the source of our true power and our authentic innocence. We are created in the image and likeness of God and indeed are redeemed by God from the power of evil and invited to share in the building of the kingdom of God.

John Paul develops his notion of the mercy of God as a power which overcomes evil. He describes the present state of the world as tottering between the potential for good or for evil. Quoting *Gaudium et Spes* he notes, "Man is growing conscious that the forces he has unleashed are in his own hands and that it is up to him to control them or to be enslaved to them."[11] In an age which has so much potential through scientific and technological means to solve special problems and alleviate human misery there exists great inequality and injustice. Here again we see the curious mixture of good and evil which marks the human condition.

> But side by side with all this (progress), or rather as part of it, there are also the difficulties that appear wherever there is growth. There is unease and abuse of powerlessness regarding the profound response which man knows that he must give. . . . All of this is happening against the background of the gigantic remorse caused by the fact that, side by side with wealth and surfeited people and societies, living in plenty and ruled by consumerism and pleasure, the same human family contains individuals and groups that are suffering from hunger.[12]

John Paul argues that justice is not enough because it will simply lead to a struggle for power. He argues for the need for mercy which contains the power of love and specifically the power of forgiveness. In relying upon the mercy of God, we are taking recognition of and responsibility for realities which are involved with power and innocence. These include the reality of evil and sin and our complicity in them, the belief that the power of God's love (as found in his mercy) is greater than the power of evil, and the realization that we are invited to share in the mercy of God. The first point (the recognition of evil and sin) relates directly to the issue of innocence which I have raised in this book. The second (the belief in the power of God's love) relates to the issue of powerlessness as an adversary of spirituality. The third point (that we are invited to share in God's mercy) brings the issue of powerlessness and innocence into the arena of our relationships with one another. "Happy the merciful; they shall have mercy shown them" (Mt 5:7). "Man attains to the merciful love of God, his mercy, to the extent that he himself is interiorly transformed in the spirit of that love toward his neighbor."[13] Thus our power comes from the love and mercy of God, and this love and mercy of God is the basis of our conversion, of our change of heart and growth in love. In regard to living this out with one another, John Paul points out that mercy is a bilateral not a unilateral reality.

> An act of merciful love is only really such when we are deeply convinced at the moment that we perform it that we are at the same time receiving mercy from the people who are accepting it from us. Then mercy becomes an indispensable element for shaping human relationships between people in a spirit of deepest respect for what is human, and in a spirit of mutual brotherhood.[14]

This reaches its height in the power human beings possess to forgive one another. "Forgiveness demonstrates the presence in the world of the love which is more powerful than sin. Forgiveness is also a fundamental condition for reconcilation, not only in the relationship of God with man but also in relationships between people."[15] It is in this context that the Christian must search out answers to the complex problems of our divided world and discover the meaning of loving one's enemies. While we have to be astute and knowledgeable about the complex forces at work in any given difficulty, we cannot expect to solve any of these problems of nuclear warfare, corporate greed, or world hunger by merely employing worldly techniques or justifying one evil because we are trying to avoid one we perceive as a greater evil. For the Christian, the challenge goes beyond the political process or the humanly expedient approach. Without being naive or unrealistic, the Christian is challenged by the cross of Christ (embodying mercy and forgiveness), a stumbling block to some and an absurdity to others.

V. Spirituality and Christian Leadership

If powerlessness and innocence are indeed adversaries of spirituality, what are some of the implications for us today? I would like to divide this into three areas: power, innocence, and tomorrow's leader.

1. Power

By the very fact of our existence we have power. This rather obvious fact needs attention because we have enough experiences of our powerlessness, of not making a difference, that we can fail to recognize that on the very basic level of existence we have power. However, we must have basic needs of our existence fulfilled or we will not be able to exercise the power of existence. Some of these needs are basic to our physical existence. They are needs of self-preservation expressed in the need for food, shelter, water, air, warmth, etc. Other needs reflect our rational and spiritual nature. These are needs of self-assertion expressed in the following areas of need: (1) the need to be accepted as a person of worth, (2) the need to ventilate my feelings to one who really listens, (3) the need for meaning in my life, (4) the need for space, and (5) the need to feel that we make a significant contribution to our group. The third are sexual needs found in a parenting role where love is seen as power and in the companion role where love is seen as passion.

These needs are basic to the experience of being human. The psychic energy behind these basic needs will seek expression. If it is thwarted on one level it will seek expression on another level. Thus, if our needs of self-assertion are thwarted, they may be displaced to the sexual area in masturbation, etc., or in the area of self-preservation as in overeating or excessive drinking. The same is true of a frustration of need in the other area and their mutual influence. The experience of powerlessness on the psychological level can be a harmful experience because it displaces psychic energy into another area. When it is done consciously and for some higher purpose, it can lead to artistic expression or creativity. But in that case it would not truly be an expression of powerlessness but an expression of power. When these needs are negated or frustrated on several levels at once, the experience of powerlessness can be especially harmful because the displacement of psychic energy can be destructive of the person.

The emotional level is very akin to this, and the same principles hold true. We all have a need to emote, to express ourselves. If we do not, if we hold things in, we will find ourselves caught in some other avenue of expression, as in drinking or in some physical manifestation such as heart problems, ulcers, headaches, etc. The basic human needs of self-affirmation, self-assertion, and self-expression are also expressions of power essential to healthy human living. We are affirmed (or reaffirmed) when we are heard even though we may still bear the same burden and feel helpless (powerlessness) to solve it. However, our experience of powerlessness on these basic emotional levels is an adversary of spirituality because it corrodes our sense of ourselves and our worth without which we cannot love.

When we speak about the spiritual level we are not talking about a new and different level. We are rather talking about the underpinnings of all that has gone before, now recognizing the presence of the human spirit and its openness to transcendence. Here we recognize our power not as a force between us but as a sharing in the creative love of a transcendent spirit. Here human dignity takes on deeper and wider proportions. And here powerlessness is an adversary of spirituality when it is a denial of God as Incarnate Spirit, when it is a denial of ourselves in our true dignity, made in the image and likeness of God.

Powerlessness is in harmony with spirituality when it is part of our acceptance of dependence upon the Lord and surrender to him. Many spiritual writers speak of our nothingness, our powerlessness as human beings, dependent upon the love and mercy of God. They reflect their own spiritual journey and the truth that, as one moves along the spiritual way into closer union with the Lord, one experiences more deeply one's own sinfulness and nothingness in the light of the infinite love and beauty of God. I think this must be carefully understood in its proper context. It can be misleading to people beginning in the spiritual life or lacking a spiritual life to make powerlessness in itself a virtue and think that they can prove their love of God by simply putting themselves down. Powerlessness as a virtue in the spiritual life is the result of a long and deep dialogue with the "Hound of Heaven." We can read the spiritual masters thinking we are understanding them, but there is a real danger of equating what I am experiencing with what they are saying, equating where I am in the spiritual life with the experience referred to by a spiritual master that, in fact, may reflect a later stage of development and depth.

At the same time the experience of powerlessness can be an opening to deeper spiritual life. It can lead us further in our dialogue with Christ and in our relationship with him. For this to happen, the experience of powerlessness must move beyond the level of human experience (where it is often a negative and frustrating experience) and become part of our reflective journey with the Lord. Then it is no longer an adversary of spirituality but an opportunity to be empowered by the risen Lord. It is, then, a process of dying and rising. The dying is a dying to self—to our false self. This is most important to understand properly because it is at the heart of distinguishing powerlessness as an adversary or an aid to spirituality. To die to oneself one has first to discover oneself and thus be able to surrender what is false or sinful in oneself. The experience of powerlessness prior to a healthy appreciation of oneself is an adversary of spirituality. The experience of powerlessness that is a surrender to the Lord whose love I recognize and accept is an aid to spirituality because it is a transformation from my powerlessness into the awesome love of God which transcends anything this world can give me.

2. Innocence

Evil exists side by side with good in this fragile, broken world of ours. This has several implications in regard to innocence. The first is to recognize that our greatest strength is also our greatest weakness, that our strongest asset is also our biggest liability. A failure to recognize this is an example of innocence as an adversary of spirituality. Great intelligence can be used to offer clarity and insight to others or it can be used to destroy them. A sense of humor can be used to give others joy; it can also be used to keep people at bay or to put them down. Generosity can bring comfort and help to people; generosity which lacks discernment can put money in the hands of a drunk.

Honesty is a good contemporary example. Honesty is to the present generation what loyalty was to a past generation. Both have their assets and liabilities and therefore are good examples of innocence and its limitations. A past generation would protect its members out of loyalty although that meant covering up and cleaning up for others to the point of contributing to their demise. In the present generation honesty is highly valued and rightly so. However, what is done in the name of honesty is too often tragic in itself. In the name of honesty people can be destroyed by a truth which they are unable to handle. In the name of honesty people can ignore the evil they are doing because they are so caught up in the fact that they are being honest about it.

Innocence wears blinders—sometimes blinders to evil within myself, at other times blinders to the evil in others, whether people, structures, or systems. Innocence wears blinders when it is so caught up in the good that it fails to recognize that this good is not an absolute good and does not stand by itself. Innocence wears blinders when it fails to recognize the complexity and complicity of good and evil within ourselves or elsewhere.

Basically, innocence is an adversary of spirituality when it fails to take account of evil. Thus the second implication: it is as important in the spiritual life to be in touch with our capacity for evil as it is to be in touch with our capacity for good. An emphasis on the one to the exclusion or even diminishment of the other leads to an impoverished spiritual life. A recognition of our goodness without an awareness of our evil leads to a naiveté which is like a house built on sand. Evil has its day most effectively when it is able to run wild because we do not recognize its presence. An emphasis on our evil and wickedness without a corresponding belief in our goodness leaves us impotent. In such a situation we justify ourselves by the evil we do not do rather than reaching out to the potential which is rightfully ours.

If we are to grow spiritually, we need to discern not only between good and evil, but also between good and not so good, good and O.K. In this broken incomplete world of ours, it is important to recognize that goodness is fragile and evil is all too real. We should ask ourselves continuously how this characteristic or that strength serves us well or serves us ill. Very often it is a question of balance and astuteness that forms the discernment so essential to personal growth.

3. The Role of Tomorrow's Leaders

By dealing with these issues in their own lives, tomorrow's leaders will be better able to address them in the lives of others. This does not mean that they will have them all sorted out. No one ever does. But if they are involved in the question of power and powerlessness and in the struggle of good and evil in their own lives, they will be able to meet another human being in a compassionate stance which leads to understanding and growth. They will be able to distinguish between authentic innocence and pseudo-innocence, as well as between real and abusive power. They will recognize innocence which is the result of grace and innocence which is the result of human blinders to evil. They will see that power itself is not evil but they will be discerning about its use. And they will recognize the importance of power in its basic sense of ability and its value in psychological and spiritual growth.

Paul Pruyser offers us a challenging perspective in his book *The Minister as Diagnostician:* "What if people have a desire to be assessed, evaluated, diagnosed by their pastor? . . . What if they want to place themselves in a pastoral-theological rather than a medical psychiatric, legal or social perspective?"[1] Spiritual leaders are not just recipients of psychiatric and medical diagnosis. They bring their own expertise, their pastoral-theological perspective, to contribute to the client's search especially where the dimension of faith is present. In the 1960's clergy were quick to refer people to the psychological and medical experts. In time they found that these professionals were sending people back and encouraging the clergy to address the spiritual transcendent dimensions of the client's experience. Ideally, in a wholistic approach, the clergy work hand in hand with the other helping professions in serving the client's needs.

Christian leaders can benefit from a willingness to listen for and appreciate the hidden meaning of events and situations as lived by people searching for meaning in their lives. Paul Pruyser speaks about this in terms of diagnosis—discerning and discriminating in any field of knowledge, distinguishing one condition from another. "To diagnose means grasping things as they really are, so as to do the right thing."[2] Tomorrow's leaders help people to name things for what they really are: to name evil as evil and to recognize the mixture of good and evil within oneself and in the fragileness of many of life's encounters. I believe that it is our role to help people to make connections in their lives (not to make the connections for them): to make connections between their human experiences and the deep longings of their spirit, to make connections between their relationships with others and their struggles within, to make connections which lead to the integration of the psychological, emotional, and spiritual dimensions of the self.

This is best accomplished through listening. People cannot be heard if no one listens. The power of listening releases the power of being heard, of being able to express oneself. And, most importantly, for that listening to be truly effective it must be a compassionate listening. Compassion is the link between power and love because compassion touches and shares deeply in the human spirit as one. Compassion is also the link between power and innocence because in compassion nothing is foreign to me and, therefore, no one is a stranger to me. Compassion, then, is the key quality of Christians who are called upon to be wounded healers and hospitable hosts.

As wounded healers they recognize that their power lies in a deep recognition of their oneness with others—in both their heights and their depths. They recognize that their wounds are a source of power for others because they enable them to listen on a deep level of their hurt, because they enable them to be present to another as a fellow traveler in pain.

Powerlessness is a reality for all of us in the face of many of life's problems and responsibilities. But our inner powerlessness can be turned into strength when we are able to transcend our external impotence by touching the depths of our own spirit. This becomes a possibility when we find hospitality in a listening, compassionate host who invites us to come and tell our story. Christian leaders trust not in answers or solutions but in the presence and significance of meaning.

In the summer of 1978, the summer of conclaves, Cardinal Manning of Los Angeles was quoted in *Time:* "Remember the old Aesop fable about the contest between the sun and the wind to get the man to remove his coat. The wind nearly beat him to death but the man only clung on more tightly. The sun warmed him a bit and the man removed his coat. That's what the Church needs to do in this era: change people through warmth."[3]

If I were asked to form Christian men and women, I would break their hearts.

Conclusion:
Compassion for the Present Moment

Since writing these reflections a year ago my
life has changed drastically. I have moved from Long Island,
New York to Rome. I have moved from one seminary where I
was very happy and deeply involved to another seminary where
I am facing the challenges of starting again. In the interim, a
month before I moved, my father died of a heart attack. Since
my mother is already deceased, his death signaled an end to a
whole world that formed my life. I had a month to sell his home
before coming to Rome. All of these circumstances have made
these past few months a very important time in my spiritual
journey—a vulnerable, delicate time.

It is, first of all, a vulnerable time, a time when I have experienced my powerlessness in a new way. All that is past seems
so much out of grasp now. All the moments for compassion
recounted at the beginning of this book are now distant memories, cherished though they be. All the memories of childhood
and family life that were touched in the experience of disman-
tling our home are now part of both my surrender and my grat-
itude to the Lord.

I have been very, very taken by the fact that my life has
changed drastically and will never be the same again. It may be
better but it will never be the same. I will never be that freckle-

75

faced boy again, but he still lives within me. I cannot go back to those life-filled days in Amityville but I will always carry in my heart the treasures I found there. I will never again be the spiritual director at the seminary in Huntington but a part of me will always be there. I have realized very deeply in these days that I not only miss having my father present but I miss being his son, an experience that I enjoyed and treasured very much. There is no longer a generation between me and death. This is not a morbid statement on my part but a very poignant realization of the passing of time and the process of purification and surrender involved in my journey to and with Christ. It is, for me, an experience of my powerlessness but a powerlessness that is leading me to the Lord because I have known his love.

The present is also a delicate time—a time when I am tempted anew, a time when innocence can be an adversary of spirituality. In the face of these changes and in the light of this powerlessness, I am tempted to substitute for the losses in my life through pride and insecurity. I am tempted to cling to others rather than to love them. I am tempted to demand that these new people in my life take my loneliness away.

I am still a very fortunate person. The God who has been faithful to me in the past has not abandoned me. Letters from home are a continual reminder that I am loved. And the marvelous people with whom I am privileged to live and work in my present circumstances give me consolation and hope about the future. Yet I experience once again the fragility of goodness. I cannot cling to these people or expect them to take my loneliness away. And I cannot merely substitute for the losses of the past. I truly believe that in the present moment the Lord is calling me beyond the grace of compassion to a deeper, starker trust in him. Perhaps, more accurately, compassion for the present moment means solitude. It is a time to simply let go and be with the Lord. This moment for compassion is beyond words and beyond the actions of service that constitute ministry. It is even beyond the experience of love and affirmation that has supported me thus far.

Experiences of brokenness and pain can lead to bitterness or compassion. They can lead to bitterness if I am not opening myself to the Lord and receiving the love and support of others. They can lead to bitterness if I experience my powerlessness with resentment that others have not met my needs. They can lead to bitterness if my innocence wears blinders and prevents me from seeing the fragileness of life. They can lead to bitterness if I am not exposing the pain to the healing presence of the Lord. But such experiences can also lead to compassion—to a solidarity with others and a unity in Christ. At times this will involve interaction with others such as the early experiences in ministry that formed me in compassion through presence to others in pain. At other times, like the present moment, it involves an inward journey—a desert of solitude with the Lord. These two basic directions are not mutually exclusive but will often exist side by side though perhaps with varying degrees of emphasis. What is most important is being faithful to the Lord in the present moment, however we discern his invitation to us. In the formation of compassion a broken heart can open to us the wisdom of God.

Bibliography

Baars, Conrad and Terruwe, Anna. *Healing the Unaffirmed.* New York: Alba House, 1976.

Frankl, Viktor E. *Man's Search for Meaning.* New York: Pocket Books, 1959.

Haughton, Rosemary. *The Transformation of Man.* New York: Paulist Press, 1967.

John Paul II. *On the Mercy of God.* Rome, 1980.

Jung, Carl G. *Modern Man in Search of a Soul.* New York: Harcourt Brace Jovanovich, 1933.

————. *Soul and Psyche.* New York: Doubleday Anchor Books, 1958.

————. *The Undiscovered Self.* Boston: Little, Brown & Co., 1957.

Kopp, Sheldon. *If You Meet the Buddha on the Road, Kill Him.* New York: Bantam Books, 1972.

May, Rollo. *Power and Innocence.* New York: W. W. Norton and Company, 1972.

Nouwen, Henri J. M. *Clowning in Rome.* New York: Image Books, 1979.

————. *Reaching Out.* New York: Doubleday and Company, 1975.

————. *The Living Reminder.* New York: Seabury Press, 1979.
————. *The Wounded Healer.* New York: Doubleday and Company, 1972.
Pruyser, Paul. *The Minister as Diagnostician.* Philadelphia: The Westminster Press, 1976.

Notes

Chapter II
1. Rollo May, *Power and Innocence* (New York, 1972), p. 99.
2. *Ibid.*, p. 100.
3. *Ibid.*, p. 106.
4. *Ibid.*, p. 109.
5. *Ibid.*, p. 111.
6. *Ibid.*, pp. 111–112.
7. *Ibid.*, p. 48.
8. *Ibid.*, p. 49.
9. *Ibid.*, pp. 49–50.
10. *Ibid.*, p. 53.
11. *Ibid.*, p. 56.
12. *Loc. cit.*
13. *Ibid.*, p. 58.
14. Rosemary Haughton, *The Transformation of Man* (New York, 1967).
15. Henri Nouwen, *Reaching Out* (New York, 1975), p. 19.
16. Rollo May, *op. cit.*, pp. 137–138.
17. Conrad Baars and Anna Terruwe, *Healing the Unaffirmed* (New York, 1967), p. vi.
18. Rollo May, *op. cit.*, p. 143.
19. *Ibid.*, p. 65.

Chapter III

1. Rollo May, *op. cit.*, p. 113.
2. *Ibid.*, p. 114.
3. *Loc. cit.*
4. *Ibid.*, p. 250.
5. *Ibid.*, p. 249.
6. *Loc. cit.*
7. *Ibid.*, pp. 251–252.
8. Sheldon Kopp, *If You Meet the Buddha on the Road, Kill Him* (New York, 1972), p. 148.
9. Rollo May, *op. cit.*, p. 166.
10. *Ibid.*, p. 260.
11. Carl G. Jung, *Psyche and Symbol* (New York, 1958), p. 7.
12. Carl G. Jung, *The Undiscovered Self* (Boston, 1957), p. 107.
13. Rollo May, *op. cit.*, p. 209.
14. *Ibid.*, p. 210.
15. *Ibid.*, pp. 210–211.
16. *Ibid.*, p. 253.

Chapter IV

1. Henri Nouwen, *The Living Reminder* (New York, 1977), p. 12.
2. Carl G. Jung, *Modern Man in Search of a Soul* (New York, 1933), p. 61.
3. Viktor Frankl, *Man's Search for Meaning* (New York, 1959), p. 30.
4. *Ibid.*, p. 56.
5. *Ibid.*, p. 146.
6. Henri Nouwen, *The Wounded Healer* (New York, 1972), p. 5.
7. *Ibid.*, p. 41.

8. Henri Nouwen, *Clowning in Rome* (New York, 1979), p. 88.

9. *Idem, Reaching Out*, p. 50.

10. *Idem, The Wounded Healer*, p. 94.

11. *The Constitution on the Church in the Modern World, Gaudium et Spes* (Rome, 1966), art. 9.

12. John Paul II, *On the Mercy of God* (Rome, 1980).

13. *Loc. cit.*

14. *Loc. cit.*

15. *Loc. cit.*

Chapter V

1. Paul Pruyser, *The Minister as Diagnostician* (Philadelphia, 1976), pp. 9–10.

2. *Ibid.*, p. 30.

3. *Time* magazine, July 1978.